T0311765

Cambridge Elements ≡

Elements in Forensic Linguistics
edited by
Tim Grant
Aston University
Tammy Gales
Hofstra University

THE IDEA OF PROGRESS IN FORENSIC AUTHORSHIP ANALYSIS

Tim Grant
Aston University

CAMBRIDGE
UNIVERSITY PRESS

CAMBRIDGE
UNIVERSITY PRESS

University Printing House, Cambridge CB2 8BS, United Kingdom

One Liberty Plaza, 20th Floor, New York, NY 10006, USA

477 Williamstown Road, Port Melbourne, VIC 3207, Australia

314–321, 3rd Floor, Plot 3, Splendor Forum, Jasola District Centre,
New Delhi – 110025, India

103 Penang Road, #05–06/07, Visioncrest Commercial, Singapore 238467

Cambridge University Press is part of the University of Cambridge.

It furthers the University's mission by disseminating knowledge in the pursuit of
education, learning, and research at the highest international levels of excellence.

www.cambridge.org
Information on this title: www.cambridge.org/9781108971324
DOI: 10.1017/9781108974714

First published 2022

A catalogue record for this publication is available from the British Library.

ISBN 978-1-108-97132-4 Paperback
ISSN 2634-7334 (online)
ISSN 2634-7326 (print)

The Idea of Progress in Forensic Authorship Analysis

Elements in Forensic Linguistics

DOI: 10.1017/9781108974714
First published online: April 2022

Tim Grant
Aston University

Author for correspondence: Tim Grant, t.d.grant@aston.ac.uk

Abstract: This Element examines progress in research and practice in forensic authorship analysis. It describes the existing research base and asks what makes an authorship analysis more or less reliable. Further to this, the author describes the recent history of forensic science and the scientific revolution brought about by the invention of DNA evidence. They chart the rise of three major changes in forensic science – the recognition of contextual bias in analysts, the need for validation studies, and a shift in the logic of providing identification evidence. This Element addresses the idea of progress in forensic authorship analysis in terms of these three issues with regard to new knowledge about the nature of authorship and methods in stylistics and stylometry. The author proposes that the focus needs to shift to validation of protocols for approaching case questions, rather than to validation of systems or general approaches. This title is also available as Open Access on Cambridge Core.

Keywords: forensic linguistics, authorship analysis, text analysis, forensic science, methods

ISBNs: 9781108971324 (PB), 9781108974714 (OC)
ISSNs: 2634-7334 (online), 2634-7326 (print)

Contents

Series Preface   1

Prologue: The Dhiren Barot Case   3

1 The Idea of the Idea of Progress   4

2 Forensic Authorship Analysis   8

3 The Idea of Progress in Forensic Science   32

4 Progress in Forensic Authorship Analysis   48

5 Future Directions in Forensic Authorship Analysis   60

Conclusions   62

References   65

Series Preface

The *Elements in Forensic Linguistics* series from Cambridge University Press publishes (1) descriptive linguistics work documenting a full range of legal and forensic texts and contexts; (2) empirical findings and methodological developments to enhance research, investigative advice, and evidence for courts; and (3) explorations and development of the theoretical and ethical foundations of research and practice in forensic linguistics. Highlighting themes from the second and third categories, *The Idea of Progress in Forensic Authorship Analysis* tackles questions within what is often seen as a core area of forensic linguistics – authorship analysis.

Authorship analysis has been a key area of interest for the author, Tim Grant, since he received his PhD in 2003. Since that time, he has contributed as a researcher on a range of interdisciplinary publications, and he has worked as a practitioner on a variety of civil and criminal cases for both the prosecution and defence. This Element, the first in our series, is a culmination of those experiences.

Drawing on these perspectives, Grant's goals here are trifold – (1) to engage with ideas from the philosophy of science in order to take a critical retrospective view of the history of authorship analysis work; (2) to describe and address key concerns of how authorship analysis work has progressed in forensic science from both stylistic and stylometric traditions; and (3) to set out an agenda for future research, including the establishment of more reliable case formulation protocols and more robust external validity-testing practices.

Given the important nature of authorship analysis in the field of forensic linguistics, we are looking forward to more upcoming Elements that will continue to enhance the discussion of best protocols and practices in the field.

Tammy Gales
Series Editor

Many persons engaged in research into authorship assume that existing theory and technology make attribution possible though perhaps elusive.

Richard Bailey
from a paper delivered at
University of Aston in Birmingham, UK
3–7 April 1978

Prologue: The Dhiren Barot Case

On 12 August 2004, at 11:20 a.m., I received a call at work from a police investigator from SO13, the London Metropolitan Police's antiterrorism branch.[1]

At the time, I was employed at the Forensic Section of the School of Psychology at the University of Leicester and I had just recently been awarded my PhD in forensic authorship analysis under the supervision of Malcolm Coulthard. The caller started by saying they had tried to find Malcolm but he was out of the country, and they went on to ask about forensic linguistics and whether I could prove a suspect had written a particular document. The caller explained they had arrested a high-value terrorist in London and unless they could prove he had written a particular document, they would have to release him in forty hours' time. They needed my help.

I quickly established that the anonymous document was about thirty pages long and that there were also a small number of comparison documents. I was told there were currently no digital versions of the documents – although if that's what I needed, I was assured, the police team would type them up at speed. Time, not resources, was the problem. I said that I could help but also that I could not possibly do this on my own. I asked if I could gather a small team. I didn't have much time; Scotland Yard was to send a fast car to pick me up which would arrive at my home in an hour and a half.

So, trying to keep the adrenaline rush out of my voice, I quickly made a round of calls. First, I recruited my University of Leicester colleague Jessica Woodhams. She is a forensic psychologist and was then in her first lecturing job having previously worked as a crime analyst at the Metropolitan Police. Jess was interested in the links between my work in authorship analysis and her work in case linkage analysis in sexual crime, and we had had a lot of useful and interesting methodological discussions. Next, I called Janet Cotterill from Cardiff University. Janet had been a PhD with me under Malcolm Coulthard and she had also had some rare casework experience. At this stage, I had only been involved in two very small cases – most of my knowledge was theoretical, not applied. I also asked Janet to recruit Sam Tomblin (now Sam Larner), who had impressed me a year before at an academic conference in mid-Wales.

I fully briefed Jess and Janet over the phone and told them to pack an overnight bag. Initially, the plan was to bring the Cardiff team to London by helicopter – in the event we all made the journey to New Scotland Yard in police cars with lights and sirens going. By 3:00 p.m., Jess and I were in a small, airless room high up in the tower block that is New Scotland Yard reading a document

---

[1] A broader description of this investigation can be found here: www.theguardian.com/uk/2006/nov/07/usa.terrorism (last accessed 19 October 2021).

entitled *The Rough Cut to the Gas Limo Project*. Janet and Sam arrived shortly afterwards, breathless and slightly sick from the journey.

I was nervous and fully aware that this case was a massive break for me personally and that it could launch my career as a forensic linguistic practitioner. I was blissfully unaware that in almost everything that had happened so far, that in almost every decision I had made, and that in almost every opportunity for a decision that had passed me by unnoticed, I had made a bad choice. With nearly twenty years of hindsight, research, and experience, I now know I had already compromised the integrity of that authorship analysis before it had begun.

This hindsight is not just personal; we should hope that with the intervening years of research into forensic authorship analysis, and into forensic science more generally, that the discipline of forensic authorship analysis should have progressed. This Cambridge Element questions the nature of progress in forensic authorship analysis and attempts to identify where, in research and practice, real progress can be claimed, and also where no progress appears to have been made. The hope is that by critically applying hindsight to research and practice in forensic authorship analysis, and through understanding progress in the broader contexts of forensic science, we can build on such progress that has been achieved. Further to this, the ambition is that by focussing attention on this idea of progress, we can accelerate improvement in the practice and the standing of the discipline.

I hope this Element reaches different audiences. The primary audience is students and researchers in forensic linguistics. I have written with advanced undergraduate and postgraduate linguistics students in mind, but also I hope students and researchers in other forensic sciences will be helped in understanding the nature, strengths, and limitations of authorship analysis evidence.

Further to this, there are of course practitioner audiences – both forensic linguistic practitioners themselves (currently a fairly limited group) and lawyers and other investigators who might want to achieve greater understanding of this form of linguistic evidence.

This text is intended as an academic text and my forays into the history and philosophy of science are perhaps of less practical use, but they are important in understanding how authorship analysis is progressing and where it has not progressed so far. I hope I can interest all these readerships in this material as much as in the more focussed discussion of authorship analysis work.

1 The Idea of the Idea of Progress

The idea of progress is itself problematic and contestable.

In 1980, Robert Nisbet wrote his important book *History of the Idea of Progress* in which he tracks the idea of progress in civilisation, thinking, and science from its origins in Greek, Roman, and medieval societies to the present day. The work originated from a shorter essay (Nisbet, 1979) before being fully developed, and in his introduction to the 2009 edition, Nisbet reasserts that 'the idea of progress and also the idea of regress or decline are both with us today in intellectual discourse' (Nisbet, 2009, p. *x*). In these works, Nisbet argues that the origins of the idea of progress for the ancient Greeks came from a fascination with what he calls *knowledge about*, and the realisation that knowledge about the world was different from other forms of knowledge (such as spiritual knowledge) in that it allowed for an incremental acquisition of this special sort of knowledge, and that this accumulation of knowledge over time led, in turn, to a betterment of life for the individual and for society.

One competing discussion to the idea of scientific progress as accumulated acquisition of knowledge is proposed in the work of Thomas Kuhn and his idea of scientific revolutions and of paradigm shifts in science. Kuhn (1962) contends that science is not merely the incremental accumulation of *knowledge about* but that it is also an inherently social enterprise and methods of science and interpretations of meanings in science undergo periodic radical shifts. Like Nisbet, Kuhn is a historian of science and of ideas, and he identifies a number of points of scientific revolution in the history of Western civilisation. These include in astronomy the shift from Ptolemaic to Copernican ideas and then the shift from Copernican to Galilean ideas, created by Keplar's and then Newton's observations and shifts in thinking. Kuhn insists that each of these shifts is not entirely based in normal science – the accumulation of *knowledge about* – but that it also involves a mix of social change and, at the particular point in time, the promise of an as-yet-unrealised greater coherence of theoretical explanation provided by the new paradigm. In each period of normal science, anomalous observations grow until the whole body of knowledge and thinking itself requires reinterpretation.

One of the most radical and controversial aspects of the Kuhnian idea of science is that of *incommensurability* between paradigms. That science carried out in one paradigm is incommensurate with science carrried out in another, puts cross-paradigm conversation beyond comprehension – the science of paradigm A cannot be engaged with or critiqued by the tools provided by the science of paradigm B or vice versa. This may suggest a strongly relativistic interpretation of Kuhn, but this is rejected by him in the final chapter of *The Structure of Scientific Revolutions* (1962), which is called 'Progress through Revolutions', and is further reinforced in a postscript to the 1970 second edition, where Kuhn suggests that a new paradigm does in fact build upon its predecessor, carrying forward a large proportion of the actual problem-solving provided by the scientific insights of that preceding work. In the second-edition postscript, Kuhn (1970) proposes that it would be possible to reconstruct the ordering of paradigms on this basis of their content and without other historical knowledge. Philosophers of science argue over incommensurability and whether it is inherently coherent, and whether it is possible to maintain as a non-relativist position (as Kuhn does). There seems to be no current consensus on these questions (see e.g. Siegel, 1987 and Sankey, 2018), but Kuhn's focus is on the *utility* of scientific insights as linking paradigms. Hollinger (1973) in a discussion on Kuhn's claims to objectivity, suggests Kuhn believes that 'Ideas "work" when they predict the behaviour of natural phenomena so well that we are enabled to manipulate nature or stay out of its way' (p. 381). This focus on ideas that work has to ground all paradigms of science, and this prevents a radical relativist position from emerging.

Focussing on utility aligns these ideas of science and progress with a further set of discussions on the nature of scientific reasoning as 'inference to the best explanation', introduced by Harman (1965). Both Kuhn's and Harman's conceptions of science are not altogether fixed but also not altogether relativistic as 'best explanations' and 'useful ideas' will change according to social contexts. Appeals to utility do seem to constrain a fully relativist position whilst allowing for scientific revolutions and paradigm shifts.

There is a final theme in discussions of scientific reasoning that links closely to the idea of 'inference to the best explanation', and this is the theme of *demonstrability*. Newton (1997) argues that scientific truths must be demonstrably true – they cannot for example be personal – but without a means of demonstration (as may be the case with spiritual truths) nor can scientific truths be private. This idea of demonstrability is one on which modern scientific practices of peer review and publication sit. The first test is that of a reviewer, who must agree that a finding has been demonstrated; the second test is that of public dissemination, where the wider community gets to consider the adequacy of that demonstration.

One area where demonstrability can create difficulty is in that of scientific prediction. Predictions need always to be grounded in first describing (or *modelling*) an evidence base. Typically, it is possible to demonstrate the adequacy of a predictive model. Most TV weather forecasts, for example, spend some time describing the status quo – what is happening with regard to high- and low-pressure systems and the locations of current storms or sunshine. Tomorrow's forecast uses this description and extrapolates. Only when tomorrow comes can the accuracy of the prediction itself be demonstrated. The science of weather forecasting can be demonstrated in terms of how often tomorrow's forecast came true – for example, my local TV station may get it right eight days out of ten.

Some predictions, however, are predictions of states of affairs which cannot be demonstrated, and these include 'predictions' of what happened in the past. To continue the example of weather predictions, it might be asked whether we can 'predict' what the weather was in a location before records began. I may want to know how wet or cold it was on the day on which the roof was completed at the Norman manor house at Aston (then Enstone) in Birmingham, UK. To make such a prediction, I need to create a model, starting with today's climate descriptions. Evaluation of the model involves looking for independent confirmation of my prediction, but there is a point at which my weather model for medieval Warwickshire is undemonstrable – it can be neither verified nor falsified – and this creates an issue as to the scientific status of such predictions. Even where the passage of time is much less than nine hundred years, demonstration of prediction of past events is difficult and needs to be done with care. One solution to this problem is termed *validation*. Validation is the demonstration that predictions can be reliable (or demonstrating the extent to which they are reliable) in cases where outcomes are known, thus demonstrating that the method is likely to be reliable where the outcome is unknown. As such, validation is an indirect form of scientific demonstration, but it may be the only form of demonstration available. An obvious problem with this idea of validation is that the known situations used to validate a model have to be as similar as possible to the situation of the prediction where the outcome was unknown. In predicting weather in the past, there is a danger that because of climate differences, modern weather models that can be validated today may be invalid in making predictions about the historic past and this will undermine the strength of the validation. These considerations are important in our contexts because a further example of predicting into the unknown past is that of casework in forensic science. In forensic science, the task in essence is to demonstrate to the courts what happened in the (typically not so distant) past. In these cases too, the issue of validation as an indirect demonstration of a scientific proposition is key, and as we shall see, the issue of whether the validation data are similar to the case data can be all important.

When considering the idea of progress in forensic science, and specifically in forensic authorship analysis, we need to consider what progress might look like. We need to ask whether there has been progress in *knowledge about* authorship and in *knowledge about* how authors' styles of writing differ from one another and how one author's style might vary over time. We need also to bring to consciousness that there may be competing paradigms for approaching authorship problems, and whether these paradigms are in fact incommensurable, or whether amounts of insight and knowledge from one paradigm can be adopted into another to create progress. We need to consider issues of utility of basic understandings about the nature of authorship for the progression of work in authorship analysis, and we need to consider issues of validation and demonstrability of results, particularly as most authorship analyses are essentially predictions about what has happened in the recent past. All of this needs to be considered when addressing the idea of progress in forensic authorship analysis.

One further thought Nisbet acknowledges is that in all cultural scientific and technological endeavours, progress is not inevitable and decline is possible. It may be that in adopting newer methods, the results may seem (or may actually be) less good than before – it also may or may not be the case that as those new methods mature, they then overtake the status quo in their utility. Decline and progress are flip sides of the same idea, and it seems incoherent to suggest that progress and not decline is possible. As well as the possibility of decline, Nisbet acknowledges that the negative consequences of progress may receive greater emphasis and create opposition to progress. As forensic authorship analysis progresses in utility, concerns over infringement of privacy may rightly increase, and progress in the area may become a victim of a catastrophic success in providing an unexpected and shocking identification of a specific individual in a high-profile controversy. Apparent progress can often be seen to catalyse opposition. Thus in 1995, a young but retired academic, Theodore John Kaczynski, published a treatise against progress which he called *The Industrial Society and Its Future*.[2] This text had significant consequences for a number of individuals whom Kaczynski maimed and killed, and it also carried implications for the progress of forensic authorship analysis.

2 Forensic Authorship Analysis

A Brief History of Forensic Authorship Analysis

It can be hard to declare the origin of any practical discipline as the practice will almost certainly have been occurring before it was noticed, labelled, and written about. In the English-speaking world, it is common to point to Jan Svartvik's (1968) short study on the language of *The Evans' Statement* with its subtitle that coined the term 'forensic linguistics'. Svartvik sets out linguistic grounds for the contention that Timothy Evans' apparent confession to the murder of his wife and baby daughter was in fact more likely authored by an interviewing police officer. Evans was hanged on 9 March 1950, convicted of the murder of his daughter (but not his wife). Just three years later, John Christie, another occupant at 10 Rillington Place, confessed to the murder of *his* wife, and was

---

[2] This was first published in the *Washington Post* and the *New York Times*, who with agreement from the FBI published it under threat of further violence – see www.washingtonpost.com/wp-srv/national/longterm/unabomber/manifesto.text.htm (last accessed 19 October 2021).

subsequently shown to be a serial murderer. This led to a re-evaluation of Evans' conviction, a number of media campaigns and appeals, and eventually Public Inquiries examining the circumstances of the Evans case. Svartvik's analysis contributed to the Public Inquiry held at the Royal Courts of Justice between 22 November and 21 January 1966 – and it is this Inquiry that finally led to Evans' posthumous pardon in October 1966.

Svartvik first discusses the issues of the transcription of Evans' spoken statement in the context that Evans has been assessed as having a 'mental age' of ten to eleven and was largely illiterate, and sets out linguistic structures that he believes were typical of Evans' language and that would persist beyond the transcription conventions of two separate police officers. Svartvik aims to be 'maximally objective: in our case this means that the features can be unambiguously stated to be open to outside inspection, and that they can be quantified and subjected to significance testing' (Svartvik, 1968, p. 24). He notes that this restricts him to high-frequency features, which in turn 'immediately rules out lexical features' (p. 25), and comments that there is no 'background material', no comparison corpus on which he can rely. He does, however, compare Evans' statements with that taken from Christie in his eventual prosecution.

As well as trying to be maximally objective, Svartvik in a footnote points out that his analysis is based firmly in linguistic research in syntax. Given his constraints, Svartvik focusses on clauses and clause types and cites the literature to support the typology he uses. Specifically, Svartvik examines the difference in distribution of relative clauses with mobile relators, where the subject can occur before or after the relator (e.g. *then* and *also* can occur as *I then* or *then I*, or *I also* or *also I*, etc.) and also elliptic subject linking clauses (which have no overt subject). He compares the statements compiled by the two police officers and creates comparisons within the statements, between sections that compromise Evans and sections that do not contain confessional material. He notes that in the crucial disputed sections of these statements, there is a significant increase in mobile relator clauses and ellipsed subject clauses associated with the police language. Svartvik states early in the report that he 'cannot hope to arrive at any firm legal conclusions; the interest of [his] study is primarily linguistic and only secondarily of a legal nature' (p. 19), and his conclusion is thus that of a correlation between 'the observed linguistic discrepancies' (p. 46) with the contested sections of the statements.

After Svartvik's contribution to forensic authorship analysis in the late 1960s, the next reports of casework in forensic authorship analysis come in the 1970s through the work of Hannes Kniffka (reported in Kniffka 1981, 1990, 1996, 2007), which reflect his work in the German language. Kniffka reports work in several cases drawing on his understandings of sociolinguistics and of contact linguistics. Of five early cases he reports from the 1970s, two are reports of disputed meaning and three are reports of disputed authorship. These relate to disputes over an article in the press, minutes of a meeting, and a particular edition of a company newsletter (Kniffka, 2007). Kniffka does not provide full details of his methods for analysis in these cases, but he does indicate the type of analysis in which he engages. For example, in the case about who wrote the edition of a company newspaper, he writes of analysis:

> On several linguistic levels, including grammar (morphology, syntax, lexicon, word order), and linguistic and text-pragmatic features, several idiosyncrasies, 'special usages', errors and deviations can be found in an exactly parallel fashion [between the disputed material and the known material].
>
> (Kniffka, 2007, p. 60)

This description suggests a broader scope in developing authorial features from a text than that applied by Svartvik, and that Kniffka brought a fuller range of linguistic knowledge and analyses to bear in this case, and presumably in other authorship cases of the time.

In the late 1980s and early 1990s, Malcolm Coulthard in the UK became involved in a series of cases which questioned the authenticity of a number of confession statements associated with serious crimes in and around the city of Birmingham. Throughout the 1980s, a regional police unit, the West Midlands Serious Crime Squad (and later the Regional Crime Squad), came under increasing pressure as it became apparent that they were involved in serious mismanagement, corruption, and demonstrated fabrication of evidence including in witness statements. In 1987, there was a turning-point case in which Paul Dandy was acquitted on the basis that a confession statement was shown to have been fabricated. The evidence for the defence came from the then novel Electro-Static Detection Analysis or ESDA technique, which is used to reveal microscopic divots and troughs left in the surface of paper by writing on it, irrespective of whether any ink stain was present. In the case of Paul Dandy, an ESDA analysis showed a one-line admission had been added to his otherwise innocuous statement, and the court released him on the basis of this evidence, but not before he spent eight months on remand in solitary confinement (Kaye, 1991). This practice of adding words to a statement to turn it into a confession became known in UK policing circles as 'verballing' and was informally acknowledged to have been a common practice of the Serious Crime Squad. A difficulty for many appeals, however, was that the original pads on which statements had been written had been destroyed. This meant that the ESDA technique could not be used and that all that remained was the language itself.

Coulthard gave linguistic evidence at a series of high-profile appeals, including the appeals of the Birmingham Six, who were convicted in 1975 of setting bombs for the Irish Republican Army (IRA) which killed 21 people and injured 182; the Bridgewater Four, who were convicted of killing twelve-year-old paperboy Carl Bridgewater by shooting him in the head after he apparently disturbed a burglary; and also at the trial of Ronnie Bolden in 1989. The Birmingham Six achieved successful appeals in 1991, the Bridgewater Four's convictions were quashed in 1997, and Bolden was acquitted. After the Bolden trial, the West Midlands Serious Crime Squad was disbanded. There were a number of other less high-profile cases from the West Midlands Serious Crime Squad and the Regional Crime Squad, to which Coulthard also contributed. He brought some of these cases to a newly formed forensic linguistic research group at the University of Birmingham. This was attended by a group of academics and PhD students including myself, Janet Cotterill, Frances Rock, Chris Heffer, Alison Johnson, Sue Blackwell, and, briefly, John Olsson. At these sessions, alongside more typical research presentations, case materials were considered, analysed, and discussed and some of the case analyses made it into Coulthard's work in investigations and in court.

In addition to these West Midlands cases, Coulthard was involved in the successful 1998 appeal of Derek Bentley's conviction. His analysis of Bentley's confession was reported in the first volume of the *International Journal of Forensic Linguistics*, now renamed *Speech, Language and the Law* (Coulthard, 1994). Coulthard's analysis uses a feature similar to that identified by Svartvik – the mobile relator – and Coulthard shows, by using corpus methods, how the *I then* form, which was present in the Bentley statement, was more typical in the police register than the *then I* form, which was more typically used by the general population – as represented by the (then impressive) 1.5 million words of the COBUILD Spoken English Corpus. This finding matched Svartvik (1968, Table 6, p. 34), where the same pre-positioned subject in *I then* appears to mark that the statement has been authored by the police officer.

Coulthard's use of corpora to understand base rates of a feature in a general population is a mark of significant progress over Svartvik – to whom the technological innovation of large, computerised corpora was unavailable, and who bemoaned the lack of ability to make proper between- and within-individual comparisons. Indeed, Svartvik notes that '[f]or a proper evaluation of the results of [his] study it would be desirable to have a better knowledge of the linguistic phenomena than we now have' (Svartvik, 1968, p. 39). He then goes on to speculate on the effect of emotional and non-emotional content on this style feature:

> It would also be valuable to know more about clause type usage generally and
> its expected range of variation in one idiolect, or, more specifically, in a
> statement made by one person on one occasion. (Svartvik, 1968, p. 39)

Svartvik is forced to rely on internal comparisons within Evans' confessions
and external comparison with the case materials of Christie's confessions in
order to provide contrast and background information. The contrast between
Svartvik's approach of using a small set of highly similar within-genre texts,
and Coulthard's approach of using a significantly sized population sample of
texts across genres remains a twin-track approach used today to understand the
distribution and distinctiveness of authorship features. As we shall see in what
follows, each has its strengths and weaknesses.

Svartvik and Coulthard, however, have plenty in common in their
approaches. They both focus on verballing in disputed confessions, and this
introduces advantages and disadvantages in their analyses. The suspect witness
statement of its time was a well-defined genre, and as Svartvik (1968) discusses,
this introduces two specific issues: the role of the police officer as amanuensis
and the introduction of features of their habitual style, and the fact itself of the
creation of a written text from the distinctive style of spoken answers. It is
through this fog of transformation that Svartvik and Coulthard are attempting to
identify the voice, the authorship, of the defendants in their cases. On some
occasions, as in Coulthard's analysis of the Bentley confession, it was sufficient
to determine that the text could not be verbatim Bentley, and that it must have
been the product of a dialogue rather than a monologue from Bentley. These
findings were contrary to the sworn statements of police officers in the original
trial and thus were considered grounds for appeal. This, however, represents a
rather indirect form of authorship analysis. On other occasions, the authorship
analysis for both Coulthard and Svartvik is more direct. Thus Svartvik suggests
that 'substandard usage', such as Evans' double negative '"She never said no
more about it"' (Svartvik, 1968, p. 22), is probably a trace of his spontaneous
speech in the statements. In both cases, however, the nature of the task
addressed and the texts analysed are working against strong, direct conclusions
of authorship.

An important and revealing but ultimately fruitless detour in the history of
forensic authorship analysis was the invention and application of cumulative
sum (CUSUM) analysis. Morton (1991) set out a graphical and apparently
general technique for spotting the language of one author inserted in a text
written by another. The plots comprised two values derived from a text plotted
in parallel sentence by sentence – typically the values were sentence length and
the number of two- and three-letter words in that sentence, although Morton,

and later Farringdon (1996), experimented with other measures (see Figure 1). An insertion of an external author was apparently revealed in a divergence of the two lines on the graph. The CUSUM technique was initially successfully used by defence teams in multiple cases including the appeal in London of Tommy McCrossen in July 1991, the trial in November 1991 of Frank Beck in Leicester, the trial of Vincent Connell in Dublin in December 1991, and the pardon for Nicky Kelly from the Irish government in April 1992 (Holmes and Tweedie, 1995, p. 20). The technique 'demonstrated' that these confession statements had been subjected to verballing and, in the McCrossen case at least, convinced the Court of Appeal that this was a wrongful conviction.

Such cases quickly attracted media attention and academic analysis which wholly discredited the technique. Holmes and Tweedie's (1995) review of the evidence cites no fewer than five published academic studies between 1992 and 1994, all of which find the technique seriously wanting (Canter, 1992; de Haan and Schils, 1993; Hardcastle, 1993; Hilton and Holmes, 1993; Sanford et al., 1994). Errors of misattribution and missed attribution were easily demonstrated. It was shown how the graph itself could be manipulated and when visual comparisons were replaced with statistical methods, no significant effects could be found to uphold the claims of CUSUM advocates. In spite of this the legacy of CUSUM in the UK lasted a decade longer. By 1998, the UK Crown Prosecutors (CPS) made a statement of official guidance that forensic linguistic

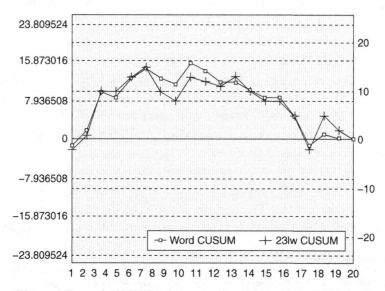

Figure 1 Example CUSUM chart reproduced from Grant (1992, p. 5) erroneously showing insertions in a text by a second author at sentences 6 and 17

evidence of authorship was unreliable, that it should not be used by prosecutors, and that it should be vigorously attacked if used by defence. This guidance was drafted to take in all forms of linguistic evidence, not just CUSUM–based authorship analysis. It was only during the preparation of the 2005 prosecution of Dhiren Barot that this guidance was narrowed to pick out only CUSUM as a demonstrably bad technique for forensic authorship analysis. This was a result of Janet Cotterill and me pointing out to the prosecutors that the negative guidance remained on the books and might undermine the case against Barot.

Even before Coulthard was untangling the confession statements written by the West Midlands Serious Crime Squad and other disreputable British police officers, forensic authorship analysis was developing in the USA. Richard Bailey (1979) presented a paper at a symposium at Aston University held in April 1978 on 'Computer-Aided Literary and Linguistic Research'. In his paper called 'Authorship Attribution in a Forensic Setting', Bailey addressed the authorship of a number of statements made by Patty Hearst, who was both a kidnap victim and also went on to join her kidnappers in a spree of armed robberies. Bailey's analysis was an early stylometric analysis – he used twenty-four statistical measures, some of which were extracted from the texts by newly written software routines called EYEBALL (Ross, 1977). It seems Bailey's analysis was not used in court but may have provided support to the prosecution legal team. It also seems likely that Bailey's contribution was the same as that presented at the 1978 Aston symposium. Further to the Hearst case, Bailey also mentions in the Aston paper that he was aware of two subsequent US trials where authorship analysis was not admitted as evidence.

It thus appears that the earliest courtroom discussion of an authorship ana-lysis in the United States was in *Brisco v. VFE Corp.* and related cross-actions in 1984. This case involved no fewer than five linguists: Gerald McMenamin, Wally Chafe, Ed Finegan, Richard Bailey, and Fred Brengelman (Finegan, 1990).[3] McMenamin provided an initial report for VFE (and its owners, Cottrell) and attributed a libellous letter to Brisco, using a method he later refers to as forensic stylistics (McMenamin, 1993). Chafe was then hired by VFE/Cottrell and affirmed that he believed that both McMenamin's methods and his conclusion were good. Finegan was then hired by Brisco's lawyers and his report was critical of the VFE's linguists' methods; he was subsequently backed up by Bailey, who examined all the available reports and supported Finegan's

---

[3] With additional information from personal communication from Professors Ed Finegan and Jerry McMenamin, including the names of the protagonists who are anonymous in Finegan (1990). My thanks go to both. Finegan is preparing a new article, which he presented at the International Association of Forensic Linguists (IAFL) conference (Finegan, 2021), and which sets out and further untangles the details of this case.

critiques. Finally, in view of the two critical reports of the original authorship analysis, VFE/Cottrell conducted a further deposition on the evidence with Brengelman as a third linguist for them, the fifth overall on this case.

The outcome of the *Brisco* case is somewhat confusing. McMenamin certainly testified at trial and his evidence went unrebutted. The fact that he went unchallenged, however, appears to be because after Brengelman's deposition and before the trial, the issue of authorship was agreed to be settled. Additionally, it appears that the whole trial, including McMenamin's evidence, was 'vacated' on grounds separate from the authorship evidence – this means the case was made void, as if the trial had never occurred. Finegan writes in personal communication that 'The judgment in the case – which included ascribing the authorship of the defamatory document as established by a linguist's expert testimony – was vacated subsequently by the very same trial judge, who later reinstated it, only to have it subsequently vacated by the California Appellate Court,' and also that then 'aspects of the case were appealed to the California Supreme Court, which declined hearing it'. McMenamin's testimony in this case seems therefore to remain vacated and to have a status akin to that of Schrödinger's cat – it was both the first instance (that I can find) of a linguist giving authorship evidence in an American court, and also, it never happened.

Irrespective of the status of McMenamin's Schrödinger's testimony, it is clear that he (along with others) went on to provide linguistic evidence of authorship in a number of cases in the late 1980s and 1990s and through to the present day.[4] Details of his approach and analysis methods are provided in two books (McMenamin, 1993, 2002). *Forensic Stylistics* in 1993 may be the first book specifically on forensic authorship analysis, and in it McMenamin reports that his approach relies on the basic theoretical idea from stylistics. This is that in every spoken or written utterance an individual makes a linguistic selection from a group of choices, and also, that in making such selections over time, the individual may habitually prefer one stylistic option over others. His method is to derive sets of features from each text he examines, often starting with the anonymous or disputed texts, and then demonstrating if these features mark the author's habitual stylistic selections in known texts by suspect authors. This stylistics basis for authorship analysis was also (somewhat unwittingly) applied as an approach in what is still one of the most high-profile authorship analysis cases worldwide – the investigation into the writings of the Unabomber.

---

[4] Professor McMenamin kindly provided me with judgments and reports for a number of his early cases.

Jim Fitzgerald, as a Supervisory Special Agent in the FBI, reports visiting Roger Shuy at Georgetown University in the summer of 1995 to hear Shuy's profile of *The Industrial Society and Its Future*, the then anonymous Unabomber manifesto (Fitzgerald, 2017). Shuy suggested that the writer of the manifesto was a forty- to sixty-year-old, that they were a native English speaker raised in the Chicago area, and that they had been a reader of the *Chicago Tribune*. As reported, Shuy's opinion was also that the writer was likely white, but he didn't rule out that he might be African-American or have been exposed to African-American Vernacular English (AAVE). Excepting this last hedging about the AAVE influence, Shuy's profile proved remarkably accurate.

The publication of the manifesto in the *Washington Post* and in the *New York Times* in 1995 resulted in the recognition by members of Theodore Kaczynski's family that the themes and the writing style in the manifesto were similar to his other writings. The family provided letters and documents received from Kaczynski, and this enabled Fitzgerald and the FBI to write a 'Comparative Authorship Project' affidavit which compared the anonymous documents with the letters from Kaczynski. The affidavit was used to obtain a search warrant for Kaczynski's remote Montana cabin. The analysis was based on more than six hundred comparisons not only of the writer's selections of words and phrases, which were '*virtually identical* word-for-word matches of entire sentences' (Fitzgerald, 2017, p. 487), but also many of which were '*somewhat similar*' and '*very similar*' across the two document sets. Fitzgerald at that time claimed no expertise in linguistics and simply presented the points in common.

In the subsequent legal challenge to the analysis, Robin Lakoff, acting for the defence, argued that these co-selections of stylistic choices were insufficient evidence to amount to 'probable cause' to support the search warrant. In response to Lakoff, the prosecution hired Don Foster, a literary linguistics expert, who defended Fitzgerald's analysis (Foster, 2000). The final judgement in this dispute was that the language analysis provided sufficient evidence to amount to probable cause, and thus the search was upheld as legal. With this finding, the considerable further written material and bomb-making materials found at Kaczynski's cabin could be admitted at trial. In January 1998, in the face of this overwhelming evidence and as part of a plea bargain to avoid the death penalty, Kaczynski pleaded guilty to the charges against him and was sentenced to life imprisonment without the possibility of parole.

Fitzgerald's work is clearly an authorship analysis and an analysis of the language evidence. That it is similar to McMenamin's stylistic approach seems to be a coincidence and may be because Fitzgerald drew on his behavioural analysis training. Behavioural analysts and psychological profilers examine crime scene behaviours to produce profiles and to link crimes committed by the same offender. In case linkage work, behaviours are coded as selections within potential repertoires of choices required to achieve different crimes (Woodhams et al., 2007). Thus, in certain sexual crimes, controlling a victim is a required aim, but this might be achieved by verbal coercion, by physical threats, by tying up the victim, or by other means. The repeated co-selection of behaviours within these repertoires can be seen as evidence that a pair of unsolved crimes may have the same offender.[5] To a degree, Fitzgerald's analysis is unusual in comparison with the analyses by the linguists Svartvik, Kniffka, Coulthard, and McMenamin. Most expert linguists would have been unlikely to comment on common content or themes across the queried and known documents, seeing this as beyond their expertise. Similarly, as linguists they would probably also have been less interested in linguistic content that was merely *very similar* or *somewhat similar*. The word-for-word matches of entire sentences, however, would still be considered strong linguistic evidence of authorship, and the idea of a set of linguistic choices identifying a specific author certainly has traction (Larner, 2014; Wright, 2017) and is referred to by Coulthard (2004) as a co-selection set.

Since the turn of the century, the growth in authorship cases has grown considerably. Perhaps building on Kniffka's early work, the German federal police (Bundeskriminalamt (BKA)) have uniquely maintained a forensic linguistic unit within the official forensic science division. Within the UK, a number of high-profile forensic authorship analyses have been taken to court, and in *R v. Hodgson* (2009), Coulthard's evidence of text messaging was appealed and his approach and opinions were upheld (Coulthard et al., 2017). There have been many more cases where authorship evidence has been provided for criminal prosecution or defence but not reached the courts. This year, a full forty-three years after Richard Bailey first spoke at Aston University on forensic authorship analysis, the Aston Institute for Forensic Linguistics held a symposium on 'International Approaches to Forensic Linguistic Casework' at which there were discussions of cases from Australia, Canada, Greece, India, Indonesia, Norway, Portugal, South Africa, Spain, Sweden, and Turkey as well as from Germany, the UK and the USA.[6]

---

[5] Interestingly, and in contrast to current UK practice in authorship analysis, there is a legal judgment (in the Scottish courts) that case linkage evidence has an insufficient scientific base to be admitted as evidence (*Young v. HM Advocate* [2013] HCJAC 145).

[6] Some of which are reported in a special issue of the journal *Language and Law/ Linguagem e Direito* (2021, 8,1). https://ojs.letras.up.pt/index.php/LLLD/index (Last accessed 25 February 2022).

A Taxonomy of Authorship Analysis

The focus in this Section is on the structure of authorship questions and the tasks which are carried out. As we have seen from its history, authorship analysis is not a unified endeavour and authorship analysis tasks vary according to the specifics of the case. As will be seen, the general term *authorship analysis* is preferred and used in contrast to *authorship attribution* as in many cases neither the aim nor the outcome of the linguistic analysis is an identification of an individual. Such analyses can roughly be broken down into three principal tasks, each of which can contain a number of sub-tasks as illustrated in Figure 2.

In Figure 2, the abbreviations Q-documents and K-documents are used to indicate Queried/Questioned documents and Known documents, respectively.

Comparative authorship analysis (CAA) can be roughly split into closed-set problems, in which there is a limited, known set of candidate authors, and open-set problems, where the number of candidate authors is unknown or very large. Closed-set problems are best classified in terms of how many candidate authors there are, from binary problems, to small, medium, and large sets of possible authors. The size of the set of candidate authors will to a great extent determine the method applied and the chances of success. Clearly defining a small set as five or fewer and a large set as twenty or more is an arbitrary distinction born out of practice, but it seems to work as a rule of thumb. Open-set problems are often also referred to as verification tasks, but in forensic work this would also include exclusion tasks. Verification tasks also occur when all documents are in fact by unknown authors and the task is to determine whether one anonymous text has the same author as a set of further anonymous texts. In problems with very many candidate authors, approaches are very different, and here are referred to as *author search* problems.

In comparative authorship analyses which are forensic, the question as to who defines the set of candidate authors is critical and different from other contexts. Scholarship in biblical, literary, and other forms of academic authorship attribution can allow the researcher to consider many types of evidence, and the scholar may engage in historical research, take into account factors such as inks or types of paper, or examine the content in terms of the psychology or opinions of the writer. All these extralinguistic factors may help determine a set of candidate authors in a specific case. When Fitzgerald investigated the Unabomber manifesto, and with his training as a behavioural analyst, he had no reason to ignore common thematic content between the known and anonymous texts or the extralinguistic forms of evidence in the case. Indeed, it was his duty to identify and evaluate all possible forms of evidence to contribute to the search for the offender. However, generally a linguist's expert role is separate

Authorship Analysis		
Comparative authorship analysis (CAA)	Closed-set authorship classification • 1 or more Q-documents • K-documents from each author	Binary problems – 2 candidate authors
		Small set of authors e.g. < = 5 candidate authors
		Medium set of authors e.g. 5–20 candidate authors
		Large set of possible authors > = 20 candidate authors
	Open-set authorship verification	Set of K-documents; 1 or more Q-documents
		Set of Q-documents; 1 or more Q-documents
		1 K-document; 1 Q-document
	Identification of precursory authorship	Comparison of 2 or more K-documents for textual borrowing or plagiarism.
Sociolinguistic Profiling	Gender profiling	
	Age profiling	
	Profiling Education/Social Class	
	Other language influence detection	[also known as Native Language Identification]
	Professional Register/Community of Practice Influence Detection	
Author Search	Q-document(s) from one author K-document(s) from very many candidate authors (greater than 100,000).	[also known as Needle-in-the-Haystack Problems, or Linguistically-Enabled Offender Identification.]

Figure 2 Taxonomy of authorship analysis problems

from that of a general investigator, and it is the police (or other investigators) who define the scope of the closed set. This also makes the police responsible for the evidence that supports the contention that there is indeed a closed set. When this occurs, this can then allow the linguist to write a conditional opinion, constraining their responsibility. For example, it might be possible to write that *of this set of authors there is stronger evidence that author A wrote the queried text than for any of the other candidate authors.*

Verification tasks (and the reciprocal exclusion tasks) occur when there might be a small set of known documents (K-documents) and a single queried or anonymous document (Q-document). The issue is whether a single Q-document has the same author as the K-documents, and these cases are structurally harder than classification tasks. One problem with these tasks is that analyses tend to express an idea of stylistic distance. This notion of distance is in fact metaphorical and there is no principled measure of how close or distant in style any two texts are, and no well-defined threshold that makes two texts close enough or far enough apart to include them or exclude them as having been written by the same author. The hardest verification task of all is one in which there is a single Q-text and a single K-text. One reason for this is that in any verification task, the K-texts have to be assumed to be representative of the writing style of the author. Although this is an assumption without foundation, it is a necessary assumption to set up a pattern of features against which the Q-text is compared. The assumption can be strengthened by the number and diversity of K-texts, but when there is just a single K-text, this is a very weak assumption indeed.

Identification of precursory authorship includes plagiarism enquiries and identification of textual borrowing that may contribute to allegations of copyright infringement. Such cases require examination of the relationships between texts, and identification and interpretation of whether shared phrases and shared vocabulary might arise independently. Such enquiries rely on the idea of 'uniqueness of utterance' (Coulthard, 2004) that accidental, exact textual reproduction between unrelated documents is highly unlikely. They are included here as a form of authorship analysis as it is often the case that the matter at question is whether a particular author really can claim a text as their own, or whether it was originally authored by someone else.

Sociolinguistic profiling is a form of authorship analysis that takes a different approach. Rather than focussing on a comparison between individuals, it focusses on social and identity variables in order to group language users. The range of possible variables is potentially enormous and has been subject to varying degrees of study, including with regard to issues discussed below of the relationships between possible essential characteristics and performed identities.[7] Nini (2015) provides a survey of the more common variables including gender, age, education, and social class, with gender being by far the most well studied. Other language influence detection (OLID) is the task of identifying which languages, other than the principal language in which a text is written, might be influencing the linguistic choices in that target language. For example, an individual might be writing in English on the Internet, but it might be possible to discover both Arabic and French interlingual features influencing that English, and this then might inform understanding of the writer's sociolinguistic history. This form of analysis is more commonly referred to as native language identification (NLI or NLID), but as Kredens et al. (2019a) point out, the idea of a single 'native' language that might be identified is problematic – many individuals are raised in multilingual environments, and some might fairly be described as simultaneous bilinguals or multilinguals with contact from several languages affecting their production of a target language. There is a further profiling task perhaps exemplified by Svartvik's and Coulthard's identification of police register in Evans' and Bentley's witness statements, or by Shuy's identification that the use of 'devil strip' indicates the writer as having linguistic history in Akron, Ohio (reported in Hitt, 2012).[8] This task is to identify a register or dialect that might indicate the community from which the author is drawn. Such a community might be a professional community, a geographic community, or a community of practice (defined by Wenger et al. (2002) as a community based in exchanged knowledge and regular shared activity). To acquire and use the identifying linguistic idiosyncrasies of such a community indicates at least strong linguistic contact with members of the community and possibly membership in it. Sociolinguistic profiling might therefore enable a linguist to draw a sketch of an anonymous offender and so assist investigators in their search for a suspect. In most jurisdictions, such profiling work will never be admitted in court and a report is typically viewed as an intelligence product rather than as evidential. Grant and MacLeod (2020) provide a discussion of the various ways forensic authorship analyses can be used outside of the provision of actual evidence in court.

Author search is a less well-studied form of authorship analysis. The task here is to devise search terms from the text of an anonymous writer, often to find online examples of other writings by the same author. These techniques might be used, for example, to identify an anonymous blogger or to link two anonymous user accounts across dark web fora to indicate that the same individual is behind

---

[7] These issues are discussed below in the sections on the Linguistic Individual and Progress in the Idea of an Author

[8] Thanks are due to an anonymous reviewer of this Element who pointed out that both Hitt and the *New York Times* fact checkers mistakenly wrote that the term was 'devil's strip' when in fact the usage is 'devil strip' as represented here.

those accounts. Or they might be used to find an anonymous dark web writer by identifying their writings on the clear web. Koppel et al. (2006b) and Koppel et al. (2011) report authorship experiments involving 10,000 authors and Narayanan et al. (2012) describe their study using a billion-word blog corpus with 100,000 authors. Using three blog posts to search, they can identify an anonymous author 20 per cent of the time and get a top twenty result 35 per cent of the time. Developments since Narayanan include Ruder et al.'s (2016) work, which provides cross-genre examples (with texts from email, the Internet Movie Database (IMDb), blogs, Twitter, and Reddit), and Theóphilo et al. (2019), who tackle this problem using the very short texts of Twitter. Kredens et al. (2019b) refer to this task in the forensic context as 'linguistically enabled offender identification' and have described a series of studies and experiments across two corpora of forum messages. In the first experiment, with a corpus of 418 million words from 114,000 authors, they first used a single message-board post as a basis for a search, and in their results, which rank likely authors from the rest of the corpus, they achieved 47.9 per cent recall in the first thirty positions in the ranking (average hit rank = 7.2, median = 4). This means that in nearly half the experiments, other posts by the anonymous author appeared in the top thirty search hits. When they took fifty randomly selected posts from the author, rather than a single post, their results improved to achieve 89.7 per cent recall in the first thirty predictions (average hit rank = 2.7, median = 1). In an even bigger experiment with a bulletin board corpus of 2 billion words from 588,000 authors, results with a single input post were reduced to 19.2 per cent recall in the first thirty predictions (average hit rank = 5.46, median = 3); and with fifty random posts from a single author as input to 45.1 per cent (average hit rank = 5.46, median = 3). These results demonstrate both the plausibility and the power of author search approaches, and the issue of increasing the size of the search pool up to a full internet-scale technology.

Across these varied authorship analysis tasks, the nature of the genre and the length of the text can be important. It perhaps goes without saying that shorter texts provide less information to an authorship analysis than longer texts, so attributing a single Short Message Service (SMS) text message may be more challenging than attributing a blog post, a book chapter, or an entire book. On the other hand, there may be several hundred or even thousands of known text messages in an authorship problem, and this can compensate for the shortness of individual messages. Grieve et al. (2019) suggest that more standard methods of authorship analysis struggle with texts of fewer than 500 words, and this can lead to approaches that concatenate very short texts. Unfortunately, this is precisely the territory in which forensic authorship analysis is situated. Ehrhardt (2007), for example, reports that for the German Federal Criminal Police Office, the average length of criminal texts considered between 2002 and

2005 was 248 words, with most being shorter than 200 words. Cross-genre comparative authorship problems, comparing, say, diary entries to a suicide note, or social media data to emails, or to handwritten letters, also raises difficulties as the affordances and constraints for different genres naturally affect the individual style. Litvinova and Seredin (2018) describe cross-genre problems as being 'the most realistic, yet the most difficult scenario, (p. 223), and there are a limited number of studies which attempt to address this issue directly (see e.g. also Kestemont et al., 2012).

Any discussion of authorship analysis requires some understanding of the process of authorship. Love (2002) writes usefully about the separate functions that occur in the process of authorship, listing precursory authorship (the dependence on prior texts and sources whether directly quoted or not), executive authorship (the wordsmithing itself in stringing together words into phrases or sentences), revisionary authorship (involving heavy or lighter editing), and finally declarative authorship (involving the signing off of a document which might be individual or organisational). These functions have been discussed in some detail in Grant (2008), but it suffices to say here that each of these functions can be fulfilled by one or more different individuals. Thus, many authors may write precursory sources used in a text, many writers might contribute actual phrases or sentences to a text, many authors may edit or change a text, and many may truthfully declare it to be theirs. Authorship attribution can only rationally be applied to texts where preliminary analysis or argument can support an assumption that a single individual was responsible for writing the text or a specified portion of it. In forensic casework, it might be reasonable to assume a single writer is involved if the queried document is a sexually explicit communication, but less so if it is a commercial extortion letter or a defamatory blog post. This reflection points to potential tasks which are currently generally unexplored in the authorship analysis literature, tasks around determining how many authors might have contributed to a text and in what ways.

Finally, there is a set of further tasks which are related to authorship analysis but which are not directly of concern here. Grant and MacLeod (2020) in their study of online undercover policing write of *authorship synthesis*, which they break down into *identity assumption*, where an individual's written presence online needs to be seamlessly taken over by an undercover operative, and *linguistic legend building*, where the task is to create a linguistic style that is sufficiently different from their own but that can be used consistently to create an online persona. In discussions of authorship disguise there are also obfuscation tasks (see e.g. Juola and Vescovi, 2011) in which the task is to hide the style of the writer as a defence against all the types of authorship analysis described in this Section.

Approaches to Forensic Authorship Analysis

In terms of broad approach, authorship analyses can be split into stylistic analyses and stylometric analyses, and both approaches can be applied to the range of tasks described earlier in this Element. The stylistic approach can be characterised as an approach where in each case, markers of authorship will be elicited from every text and thus the markers of authorship will vary from case to case. In contrast, stylometric approaches attempt validation of markers of authorship in advance of tackling a specific problem and thus hope to create a set of general reliable measures of any author's style. Neither stylistic nor stylometric approaches necessarily require a manual analysis or a computational approach, but typically stylistic approaches tend to be associated with hand analysis and stylometric approaches with computational analysis. Since its origins, forensic authorship analysis has involved the descriptive linguistic and statistical approaches, as exemplified by Svartvik, and computational techniques, as foreshadowed in Bailey's computer-assisted analysis and in Coulthard's corpus work in the Bentley case. Stylistic and stylometric approaches are sometimes seen as in opposition to one another, and possibly from incommensurable paradigms, but again, as exemplified by Svartvik and Coulthard, this does not have to be the case.

When considering the question of progress in forensic authorship analysis, this might address different aspects of the tasks which can be seen as three categories of research:

(1) **The linguistic individual**: questions of why there might be within-individual linguistic consistency and between-individual linguistic distinctiveness, and to what extent any or all of us possess a discernible 'idiolect';

(2) **Markers of authorship**: questions about the best methods to describe texts and to draw out any individuating features in those texts (sometimes referred to as markers of authorship), and about the best methods for partialing out influences on style other than authorship – for example, from the communities of practice from which an author is drawn, from genre, or from the mode of production of a text;

(3) **Inference and decision-making**: questions about the best methods to draw logical conclusions about authorship and how to weigh and present those conclusions.

Each of these areas is now addressed.

The Linguistic Individual

Discussions of the linguistic individual often begin with the idea of idiolect. Originating with Bloch (1948) and then Hockett (1958), the concept of 'idiolect' indicated a pattern of language associated with a particular individual in a particular context. It has been developed in contemporary forensic linguistic discussions, which often begin with the well-cited quotation from Coulthard that

> The linguist approaches the problem of questioned authorship from the theoretical position that every native speaker has their own distinct and individual version of the language they speak and write, their own idiolect, and ... this idiolect will manifest itself through distinctive and idiosyncratic choices in texts. (Coulthard 2004, p. 432)

This raises empirical questions as to whether what Coulthard asserts is true, or partly true, and theoretical questions as to whether it has to be true to provide a sound foundation for forensic authorship analysis. Grant (2010, 2020) distinguishes between population-level distinctiveness, which aligns with Coulthard's theoretical position here, and pairwise distinctiveness between two specific authors, which does not require that 'every native speaker has their own distinct and individual version of the language'. Authorship analyses which rely on population-level distinctiveness require large-scale empirical validation projects to demonstrate how select baskets of features can fully individuate one author from any others. Other forms of authorship analysis, though, with smaller sets of potential authors, need only rely on distinctiveness within that group or between pairs of authors in that group.

Further theoretical questions arise as to what might explain both within-author consistency and between-author distinctiveness. Grant and MacLeod (2018) argue that these might be best explained through the idea that the individual draws on identity resources which both provide linguistic choices and constrain the choices available to them. These resources include relatively stable resources such as an individual's sociolinguistic history and their physicality in terms of their physical brain, their age, biological sex, and ethnicity (which index their identity positions relative to others and so shape their linguistic choices). Alongside these are more dynamic resources which explain within-author variation such as the changing contexts or genres of interactions and the changing audiences and communities of practice with which they engage. Such discussions raise the further possibility that some individuals might be more distinctive than others, and this is provided some empirical support by Wright's (2013, 2017) study of emails in the Enron corpus and has implications for the practice of authorship analysis and for the validation of methods of authorship analysis.

Markers of Authorship

The distinction between stylistic and stylometric approaches tends to drive the type of linguistic features which are considered as potential markers of authorship for use in an analysis.

As might be expected when asking a stylistician to examine a text, features are observed from what Kniffka (2007) refers to as different 'linguistic levels' (p. 60). Kniffka refers to grammar, linguistic, and text-pragmatic features as well as idiosyncrasies, 'special usages', errors, and deviations. Further to this, McMenamin (1993) in his impressive appendices provides annotated bibliographies of descriptive markers and quantitative indicators of authorial style. These are grouped into types of features in terms of

- usage (including spelling, punctuation, and emphases and pauses indicated in writing);
- lexical variation;
- grammatical categories;
- syntax (including phrasal structures, collocations, and clause and sentence structures);
- text and discourse features (including narrative styles and speech events, coherence and cohesion, topic analysis, introductions, and conclusions);
- functional characteristics (including proportion of interrogatives vs declaratives);
- content analysis;
- cross-cultural features; and
- quantitative features of word, clause, and sentence length, frequency, and distributions.

Grant and MacLeod (2020), following Herring's (2004) approach to computer-mediated discourse analysis, group authorship features as:

- structural features (incorporating morphological features including spelling idiosyncrasies, syntactic features, and punctuation features);
- meaning features (including semantic idiosyncrasies and pragmatic habits);
- interactive features (openings and closings to messages and including turn-taking and topic-control); and
- linguistic features indicative of social behaviours (such as rhetorical moves analysis as applied to sexual grooming conversations (see e.g. Chiang and Grant, 2017).

Whilst there are differences in principles of organisation between these groupings of features, one thing they all have in common is an attempt to move above structural-level features of word choice, syntax, and punctuation.

Understanding authorship style in terms of a text's organisation, meanings, and functions also allows a rich, multidimensional description of a text, which may allow a description of what Grant and MacLeod (2020) refer to as a 'complete model of the linguistic individual' (p. 94). Grant and MacLeod also suggest that the higher-level linguistic features go less noticed by writers and therefore might be where individuals leak their true identities when attempting authorship disguise.

In contrast, and with some notable exceptions, stylometric studies tend to focus on features from the 'lower' structural levels of language description. There have been a series of reviews of stylometric features. Grieve (2007) examines various features including the frequency and distribution of characters (specifically alphabetical characters and punctuation marks) and words. He also tests a set of vocabulary richness measures, the frequency of words in particular sentence positions, and the frequency of collocations. Finally, Grieve examines character-level n-gram frequency (from bi-grams to 9-grams).

N-gram measures are frequently used in stylometric studies and simply take each sequence of units that arise from a text. Grieve (2007) examines character n-grams, but other researchers also use word n-grams and parts-of-speech n-grams. These are sometimes referred to as character-grams, word-grams, and POS-grams, respectively. Thus, taking an extract from Dickens' famous opening to *A Tale of Two Cities*:

> It was the best of times, it was the worst of times, it was the age of wisdom, it was the age of foolishness …

In this portion, we can extract the character sequence 'it_was_the_', which can be counted three times as a character 11-gram. The initial occurrence 'It_was_the_' (beginning with the uppercase 'I') isn't within this count, but the shorter 10-gram 't_was_the_' does occur four times. In this example, the capitalisation of 'I' is counted as a different character, but a decision could be made to ignore capitalisation. Additionally, the same stretch of text, 'it_was_the_', could count as a word 3-gram with four occurrences, or indeed a part-of-speech 3-gram (pronoun-verb-determiner) also with four occurrences. It is important to note of analyses that extract all n-grams from a text that these n-grams may or may not carry interpretable linguistic information. Thus, in the Dickens text, the character 2-gram 'es' has three occurrences, but it is difficult to argue that this textual signal carries truly linguistic information. If, on the other hand, you calculate all character 2-9-grams from a text, then you can expect that some of these will pick up understandable linguistic markers such as the regular use of morphological features in a text indicating a preferred tense by one author, or a characteristic use of a prepositional 'of' over the genitive apostrophe by another author.

That character n-grams can both be very useful as authorship features and also have no linguistic meaning can be a real issue in forensic authorship analyses. The problem is that of explicability in court. An expert witness who can describe and fully explain what it is that one author does that a second author does not do adds not only credibility to their testimony, but also validity to their analysis in terms of providing demonstrable truths. Without linguistic explanation of features, there can be an over-reliance on black-box systems, equivalent to reliance on mere authority of an expert witness in court. This is only partially countered by well-designed validation studies. Limitations of approaches that use opaque features and methods are picked up in the Section on Progress in Stylistics and Stylometry.[9]

In his study, Grieve (2007) finds that character n-grams (up to about 6-grams) can be useful as authorship markers along with various measures of word and punctuation distribution, and shows how with a decreasing number of candidate authors in a closed set, other features, including some measures of lexical richness and average word and sentence length, might have some role to play, but generally lack a strong predictive power.

Stamatatos (2009) also provides a survey of stylometric authorship analysis methods; although his interest is more in the computational processes used in combining features and producing outcomes rather than the features themselves, he does use a very similar set of features to Grieve. These include:

- lexical features including word length, sentence length, vocabulary richness features, word n-grams, and word frequencies;
- character features including n-grams and character frequencies (broken down into letters, digits, etc.);
- syntactic features based on computational part-of-speech tagging and various chunking and parsing approaches; and
- semantic features such as synonyms and semantic dependency analysis.

Stamatatos does not specifically provide a feature-by-feature evaluation, but he does comment that in stylometric work, the most important criterion for selecting features is their frequency. Essentially, without large counts of features there is insufficient potential variability between authors for stylometric algorithms to find points of discrimination. This computational hunger for bigger counts of features, and so distributional variance between authors, drives not only the

---

[9] A relatively unexplored possibility in the research literature is to actively use character n-gram analysis as a linguistic feature-finding method. It is quite possible to start with a complete list of character n-grams from a set of problem texts, to examine them to see which has potential linguistic explanation, and then to carry out analysis to observe any reduction in performance that occurred from omitting the 'meaningless' features.

types of feature, but also a requirement of sufficient length of text. Furthermore, Stamatatos cites Koppel et al. (2006a) who suggest that the mathematical *instability* of features is also important. This refers to features where there is more linguistic affordance for choice between alternatives (within a particular genre of text), which are thus more likely to create usable markers of authorship.

Argamon (2018) explicitly acknowledges that in feature selection for computational stylometric analyses there is a compromise:

> Choice of such features must balance three considerations: their linguistic significance, their effectiveness at measuring true stylometric similarity, and the ease with which they can be identified computationally.
>
> Argamon (2018, p. 25)

He acknowledges that some linguistically meaningful features such as metaphor are not yet sufficiently computationally tractable and points to a classic feature, the relative use of function words, as the kind of feature that does meet these criteria. Function word analysis originates with Mosteller and Wallace's (1964) classic study of the authorship of *The Federalist Papers* and are now included in many current stylometric studies. Argamon further points out:

> Function word use (a) does not vary substantially with topic (but does with genre and register) and (b) constitutes a good proxy for a wide variety of syntactic and discourse-level phenomena. Furthermore, it is largely not under conscious control, and so should reduce the risk of being fooled by deception.
>
> Argamon (2018, p. 26)

Using function words to point to discourse-level phenomena is similar to the route Argamon takes to provide more linguistically informed features. Argamon and Koppel (2013) show how function words like conjunctions, prepositions, and modals (amongst others) can be used in authorship problems and then can be interpreted as linguistically meaningful features in a systemic functional context. A similar approach is taken by Nini and Grant (2013), who suggest that such a tactic can bridge the gap between stylistic and stylometric approaches to authorship analysis, and by Kestemont (2014), who argues that function words can usefully be reinterpreted as *functors* to create linguistically explicable features.

Stylometric methods thus tend to use a fairly small and closed set of features across authorship problems (although n-gram analysis might be seen as a method for generating many features from a text). This has meant that much of the focus in stylometry has shifted to the methods of decision-making through the application of different computational approaches to the classification of texts. Stylometry has given rise to a series of authorship competitions run by an academic collective under the umbrella of PAN (https://pan.webis.de) and although in PAN competitions there is some variation in the baskets of features used by different teams addressing different problems, the overlap between feature sets is more striking. Evidence from PAN suggests that the current idea of progress in computational forensic authorship analysis tasks will come from better classifiers and deep-learning approaches (or perhaps approaches that enable fuller understanding of the classifications), rather than progress in broadening the features that might be indicative of authorial style. In contrast, stylistic analysis might be criticised for allowing too much variation in both features and methods between analysts. Feature elicitation from texts requires a more rigorous protocol for deriving features, and more rigour is required for making authorship decisions on the basis of those features. For both approaches there needs to be a greater focus on protocols that will ensure that the features extracted can discriminate between authors, rather than between genres, registers, or topics of texts. This is an issue to which we return.

Inference and Decision-Making

The principal purpose of Mosteller and Wallace's (1964) book into the authorship of *The Federalist Papers* was not the authorship question per se. The focus in fact was on how Bayesian approaches to likelihood could be used in making complex decisions such as authorship questions. As they wrote later:

> A chief motivation for us was to use the Federalist problem as a case study for comparing several different statistical approaches, with special attention to one, called the Bayesian method, that expresses its final results in terms of probabilities, or odds, of authorship. (Mosteller and Wallace, 1989, p. 121)

This focus on methods of decision-making has followed through into much stylometric research. As noted earlier in this Element, the principal innovation across most of the PAN studies has been in methods of decision-making in terms of using advanced algorithmic techniques. This innovation includes novel ways to measure textual similarity or difference and innovation in the application of machine-learning and classification techniques to answer various authorship problems. Argamon (2018) provides a discussion of such techniques for the non-expert and points out that the analyst should not make assumptions that methodological trials generalise to real-world authorship attributions, but analysts need to 'evaluate the chosen method on the given documents in the case' (p. 13).

One aspect of stylistic authorship analysis work is that the inferential process by which decisions are made is sometimes somewhat opaque and that there is considerable variation between researchers. Svartvik (1968) uses a basic statistical analysis in his study of the Evans statement and McMenamin (1993) points to Bayesian statistical methods as a way forward. Grant (2010, 2013, 2020) introduces the use of the Jaccard coefficient as a way of measuring stylistic difference (for short texts with features coded as present/absent in each text) and then demonstrates inconsistency of style between authors using a series of Mann–Whitney tests. In many stylistic cases, however, including in the Barot case in the UK, in both the Brisco and the Unabomber cases in the USA (and potentially also in Kniffka's early authorship cases), and in many more recent cases, there is a focus on arguing from the evidence presented rather than an interest in formal decision-making methods.

In addition to this, and for both stylometric and stylistic approaches, little attention is paid to protocols for approaches to different authorship analysis problems. Such protocols might include initial evaluation of the problem and texts, decision-making procedures for elicitation or selection of authorship features, decision-making as to which approaches or algorithms can be selected to determine answers to the questions, and finally decision-making as to how conclusions should be expressed. There are some exceptions with Grant (2013), Argamon (2018), and Juola (2021) offering potential for deriving protocols for some aspects of stylistic and stylometric approaches, respectively.

The Ethics of Forensic Authorship Analysis

A further area which requires considerable development is in thinking through the ethics of forensic authorship analysis. The starting point has to be that nearly all authorship analyses constitute an intrusion into the privacy of an individual and that this requires justification. This is true whether that individual is a novelist writing under a pseudonym, such as Eleanor Ferrante or Robert Galbraith, or whether the analysis is of a username of an individual on a dark web site set up to exchange indecent images of children. Authorship analysis is neither morally neutral nor inherently constrained in its application. It can be used as a necessary and proportionate method to protect individuals and society from a variety of harms, or it might be used to identify and potentially do harm to whistle-blowers or political activists of one persuasion or another.

One interesting development in security ethics which might apply to authorship analyses is the 'ethical liability model' developed by Nathan (2017). Nathan, in considering the ethics of undercover policing, suggests a departure from the simplistic dichotomy between rules-based and utilitarian models of ethics to one that addresses the location of the liability for certain types of wrong. Nathan is dissatisfied with utilitarian justifications of deception and manipulation in undercover policing as he says it leaves an 'ethical residue' with those undercover police officers. In a legal and well-justified undercover operation, police officers might be asked to deceive and manipulate, and Nathan contends that these are still wrongs even if they carried out for the greater good. He argues that in these situations, the liability for the wrong, the ethical residue for wrongdoing, can be placed with the offenders. He argues that this is similar to a situation in which an attacker is killed by a defender in an act of self-defence. The defender is well justified, but harm has still been done. Nathan locates the responsibility for this harm with the attacker.

Similarly, then, intrusion against an anonymous abuser *is* still intrusion, but the responsibility for that intrusion is theirs, created by the actions and harms of their cause. The responsibility for the intrusion done to a pseudonymous novelist, against whom there is no issue of liability, thus lies squarely with the authorship analyst. Clearly there needs to be considerably more thinking with regard to the issues of authorship analysis as an intrusion and where and how it might be justified, and such discussions are well beyond the scope of this Element, but Nathan's work provides a useful starting point.

Conclusions

With regard to the Barot case, no computational analysis was possible within the constrained time period and circumstance, and thus it is unsurprising that the analysis was a stylistic analysis. In terms of taxonomy, it was a verification task – we had a small selection of known writings from Barot to compare with the twelve-thousand-word query text, *The Rough Cut to the Gas Limo Project*. The feature set was broad: there was no pre-planned protocol to elicit features and no formal validation of method or features. Subsequent to the initial analysis, we carried out work to demonstrate rarity of these features, but the overall analysis fell a long way short of current understandings of forensic science.

3 The Idea of Progress in Forensic Science

A Brief History of Forensic Science

Just as it is difficult to spot the origins of forensic authorship analysis, so it is difficult to plot an absolute origin point for forensic science. A fascinating early text is Song Ci's 1247 book *Collected Cases of Injustice Rectified*, also known as *The Washing Away of Wrongs*. Song Ci was a judge and coroner interested in autopsy and medical examination in Hunan Province in China during the middle of the thirteenth century. He made detailed observations to distinguish causes of death. For example, he described post-mortem features of bodies of people who had died by drowning, by suffocation, and/or by strangulation (but these recognisably scientific observations appear along-side descriptions of bodies of individuals who had died from fear of goblins). In terms of *knowledge about*, forensic pathology has moved on considerably since thirteenth-century China, but Song Ci's messages about the purpose and ethics of forensic examination are pertinent today. He writes:

> If an inquest is not properly conducted, the wrong of the murdered man is not redressed, new wrongs are raised up amongst the living, other lives sacrificed, and both sides roused to vengeance of which no man can foresee the end.
>
> Song (2010, p. 5)

One significant message of the book is that the success of an inquest depends as much on the integrity of the individual coroner as on their knowledge and skill.

Many histories of forensic science in the Western world begin with the advent of analytic chemistry, fingerprinting, and photography in the 1800s, and with the coincident origins of professional policing and the rise of the role of the detective in different parts of the world. The rise of forensic toxicology was marked in France with the 1813 publication of *Traite de Poissons* by Mathieu Orfila from the University of Paris, the 1835 resolution of a case by Henry Goddard of the London Bow Street Runners using the comparison of bullet moulds, and the 1880 *Nature* publication of an article on forensic fingerprinting by Henry Faulds. This rise of the forensic sciences culminates with Edmond Locard's statement of his Exchange Principle that 'every contact leaves a trace', which was attributed to him but which he may never have said. The closest expression seems to be

> La vérité est que nul ne peut agir avec l'intensité que suppose l'action criminelle sans laisser des marques multiples de son passage.[10]
>
> (Locard, 1920, p. 139)

Nevertheless, the twentieth century saw the subsequent accumulation of *knowledge about* across forensic science disciplines which apparently demonstrated the truth of his aphorism.

In 1987 came a turning point that marks a significant shift in forensic science across many cases – the development of the use of DNA as evidence of identity. This development arguably produces a paradigm shift not only in the analysis of human secretions and deposits, but also in forensic science more generally. In 1987, Colin Pitchfork was convicted for the rape and murder of Lynda Mann in Narborough, Leicestershire, in the UK, and of Dawn Ashworth in Enderby, a

---

[10] The truth is that no one can act with the intensity that criminal action supposes without leaving multiple marks in its passage.

few miles away (Evans, 1998).[11] The first use of DNA profiling evidence in this investigation in fact proved the innocence of the then prime suspect for these murders. At interview, Robert Buckland, a seventeen-year-old with learning difficulties, had knowledge about the position of Dawn Ashworth's body and then confessed to her murder, although he consistently denied murdering Lynda Mann. Alec Jeffreys of the University of Leicester (building on the work of Peter Gill and Dave Werret of the UK's Forensic Science Service) produced the world's first DNA profile to be used in a criminal investigation.[12] This demonstrated that semen taken from Ashworth's body was not Buckland's, and also that the two murders were indeed carried out by the same offender. Without the DNA evidence, it would have been highly likely that Buckland would have been convicted, but instead the investigation had to continue. During a community collection of five thousand DNA samples, Pitchfork got a friend to provide a sample in his stead, but this deception was discovered and Pitchfork was ultimately identified as having the same DNA profile as the secretions left on the bodies of the two fifteen-year-olds. This was a great step forward in forensic analytic techniques and in *knowledge about* how to place an individual at a crime scene that radically transformed the power of forensic science to solve old, cold cases as well as new. From the 1990s the growth in the use and sophistication of DNA evidence was rapid, and it brought justice to many victims of crime through bringing convictions of the guilty. Building on the demonstration of Buckland's innocence, it also brought justice through exonerating many victims of mistaken conviction, not least through initiatives such as the Innocence Project, which was established just five years after the conviction of Colin Pitchfork.[13]

The creation of DNA profiling as a forensic science technique and the growing realisation of the strength and scientific soundness of DNA evidence led to a reappraisal of other forensic sciences. In this sense, 1987 marks the beginning of a scientific revolution for forensic identification sciences (Saks and Koehler, 2005) and the point at which forensic sciences themselves become the subject of intense scrutiny. This scrutiny has led to significant change in how

---

[11] On a personal note, the crimes are local to me. I live just a few miles from the sites of these murders and a few miles from the village of Newbold Verdon, where Pitchfork grew up. In June 2021, in spite of local concerns and campaigns against his release, the Parole Board agreed that after serving thirty-three years, Pitchfork should be released into the community under tight restrictions. This decision was appealed by the Justice Secretary but was upheld in a judge-led review. On 1 September 2021, Pitchfork was therefore released on parole but in November 2021, he was recalled for approaching young women in the street, thereby breaching his release conditions.

[12] In 1985, Jeffreys had used the technique in an immigration hearing to support the asserted relationship between a mother and her son.

[13] https://innocenceproject.org (last accessed 19 October 2021)

expert scientific evidence is researched, how evidence in individual cases is evaluated, and how experts are perceived in the courtroom. The change created by DNA evidence is more than the acquisition of new *knowledge about*; the change has created a reframing of the nature of forensic science and of the role of the expert scientific witness.

Recognition of Three Issues

Two decades after the use of DNA evidence in the Pitchfork case, the discrepancy between the explicit scientific foundation for DNA evidence and the apparent lack of foundation in other sciences was attracting the attention of governments and legislators. In the United States, Congress requested that the National Academy of Science (NAS) take evidence and report on the state of forensic science in the United States. The 2009 report begins by recognising that 'the forensic science system, encompassing both research and practice, has serious problems' (NAS, 2009, p. xx). It sets out the context of forensic science as a set of interpretative disciplines and states that the 'simple reality is that the interpretation of forensic evidence is not always based on scientific studies to determine its validity', and also that 'there is a notable dearth of peer-reviewed, published studies establishing the scientific bases and validity of many forensic methods' (pp. 7–8). Further to this, the report states that for disciplines "that rely on subjective assessments of matching characteristics … these disciplines need to develop rigorous protocols to guide these subjective interpretations and pursue equally rigorous research and evaluation programs' (p. 8). The NAS report concludes:

> With the exception of nuclear DNA analysis, however, no forensic method has been rigorously shown to have the capacity to consistently, and with a high degree of certainty, demonstrate a connection between evidence and a specific individual or source. (p. 7)

In the UK, the House of Commons ordered a Law Commission examination of Expert Evidence (2011) which also criticised the reliability of forensic science evidence. The commission recommended a new admissibility test for expert evidence and a proper framework for screening expert evidence in criminal proceedings. It also produced a draft bill to put these changes into effect. Although the bill and approach were officially rejected by the Ministry of Justice in 2013, the Criminal Procedure Rules Committee adopted some of the recommendations, and these Rules have the force of secondary legislation. Further to this, in 2019, the UK House of Lords Science and Technology Select Committee published a report subtitled 'A Blueprint for Change' and the report is blunt, summarising baldly that 'the quality and delivery of forensic science in England and Wales is inadequate' (House of Lords, 2019, p. 4). It finishes with the recommendation that the UK 'urgently and substantially increase the amount of dedicated funding allocated to forensic science for both techno-logical advances and foundational research' (§187). As with the NAS (2009) report and the Law Commission report (2011), there is the recognition of twin problems – of ensuring the validity of the basic science, and of recognising and eliminating potential for bias and error in interpretation. With regard to ensuring validity, this is a call for an increase in *knowledge about*. The call for validation is initially a call for basic science in each forensic discipline to build a know-ledge base on which forensic techniques can sit. Eliminating bias, on the other hand, is more of a call for a change in thinking about how forensic analyses are carried out.

Finally, a third issue can be identified in the UK reports (which is not addressed in the NAS report): a focus on the thinking about the *logic* of forensic evidence, about decision-making on the basis of scientific evidence. Thus the Law Commission (2011) proposed a change to Criminal Procedure Rules that an expert report should include:

> a rule that where an expert witness is called by a party to give a reasoned opinion on the likelihood of an item of evidence under a proposition advanced by that party, the experts report must also include, where feasible, a reasoned opinion on the likelihood of the item of evidence under … alternative propositions. (p. 113)

Each of these three issues is now discussed in more detail.

The Issue of Validation

The 2009 NAS report was followed up in 2016 by the President's Council of Advisors on Science and Technology (PCAST), which provided a report on 'Ensuring Scientific Validity of Feature-Comparison Methods' (PCAST, 2016) in which the theme of validation was particularly identified and discussed. The stated aim as expressed in the executive summary was to fill two important gaps:

> (1) the need for clarity about the scientific standards for the validity and reliability of forensic methods
> (2) the need to evaluate specific forensic methods to determine whether they have been scientifically established to be valid and reliable. (p. 1)

The report focusses on a series of feature comparison methods (DNA sam-ples, bite marks, latent fingerprints, firearm marks, footwear, and hair comparisons). Throughout the report the authors find the non-DNA disciplines wanting, writing disparagingly about the lack of validation studies. Having expressed considerable concern for the state of forensic science generally, they set out criteria for testing the 'foundational' and 'applied' validity of forensic science methods, where 'foundational' validity refers to the basic scientific studies and 'applied' validity to the application protocols for specific cases. Foundational validation can be seen as demonstrating that predictions can be reliably made on the basis of a specified method in general problems. Applied validation is required to demonstrate reliability of prediction within narrowly defined parameters of specified forensic problems.

On foundational validity PCAST (2016) asserts that:

> (1) Foundational validity. To establish foundational validity for a forensic feature-comparison method, the following elements are required:
>
>   (a) a reproducible and consistent procedure for
>
>   (i) identifying features in evidence samples;
>
>   (ii) comparing the features in two samples; and,
>
>   (iii) determining, based on the similarity between the features in two sets of features, whether the samples should be declared to be likely to come from the same source ('matching rule'); and
>
>   (b) empirical estimates, from appropriately designed studies from multiple groups, that establish
>
>   (i) the method's false positive rate – that is, the probability it declares a proposed identification between samples that actually come from different sources; and,
>
>   (ii) the method's sensitivity – that is, the probability it declares a proposed identification between samples that actually come from the same source. (p. 65)

PCAST (2016) finds that there are sufficient studies to support foundational validity in some forms of DNA analysis and (to a lesser degree) for latent fingerprint examination, but no such foundational validity had been established for bite-mark analysis, firearms analysis, footwear analysis, or hair analysis, and for other forensic disciplines there is an assumption that they are no further advanced as 'many forensic feature-comparison methods have historically been assumed rather than established to be foundationally valid based on appropriate empirical evidence' (p. 122). Forensic authorship analysis is not considered.

The PCAST report has received some criticism from the US Department of Justice (DOJ, 2021). This response takes exception to the idea that all feature comparison requires measurement, arguing that many forms of comparison result in nominal categorisation (such as biological sex and colour) rather than measurement per se, pointing out that some properties of a phenomenon have no magnitude and so cannot be subject to metrical evaluation. The report's authors point to the *Kuhmo Tire* decision, which is that 'an expert testimony may – but need not be – derived from or verified by measurement of statistics' (p. 7). Secondly, the DOJ critiques the narrow definition of validation adopted by PCAST, arguing that there is no *single* scientific method to validate findings. The DOJ rejects PCAST's six criteria for evaluating studies and instead points to ISO17025 (the International Organization for Standardization (ISO) criteria for assessing the competence of testing and calibration laboratories) which allows for a variety of methods for validation. Finally, the DOJ objects to the idea that there is a single form of error rate that can only be established using black-box studies, citing Thompson et al. (2017) on fingerprinting, who point out that error rates can vary enormously according to a variety of factors such as the 'quality of the prints, the amount of detail present, and whether the known print was selected based on its similarity to the latent print' (p. 45). The DOJ here is making the point that the number of variables and the interactions between them cannot always be reduced to simple and informative error rates, that foundational validity is not enough.

The UK Forensic Science Regulator's Guidance on Validation in 2020 sets out the requirements for satisfactory validation studies. Just as the PCAST report distinguishes between 'foundational validity' and 'applied validity', the Forensic Science Regulator (FSR) draws a different distinction between 'developmental validation' and 'internal validation' (FSR, 2020, § 6.2.7), with the latter referring to the validation of a method as it is applied within a particular laboratory. In a further, related distinction, Morrison (2018) and Morrison et al. (2021) point to an issue of validity in forensic speech science and argue convincingly that, in speech science at least, case-specific adjustment of validation results is also required. They refer to this as 'calibration'.

Although the FSR writes, 'It is not part of the role of the Regulator to become directly involved in the validation of new methods within the field of forensic science' (§10.1.1), and although she does indeed follow ISO17025 and takes a broader view of validation studies than PCAST, she also sets out a framework for a successful validation of a method and then its application in a forensic laboratory (FSR, 2020, §7.1.1). The wider report provides a detailed protocol for carrying out such studies both on the basic techniques and on the establishment of the competence of a particular forensic unit in carrying out any such study.

In spite of these calls from both the USA and the UK, across the forensic sciences, the rate at which validation studies are occurring is slow. The UK FSR manages to cite four cases where lack of validation was seen as an issue at criminal appeal, but forensic evidence of all sorts is still used in the English and Welsh courts every day. There is a similar picture across the fractured jurisdictional landscape of the USA (DOJ, 2021), but there are also examples of good practice. Even the PCAST report commends the FBI laboratory's research programme on latent fingerprint examination, saying it is:

> an example of important foundational research that it was able to carry out incrementally over a five-year period … leading to an important series of publications [and that] [s]imilar lines of research are being pursued in some other disciplines, including firearms examination and questioned documents.
> (PCAST, 2016, p. 132)

One aspect of the debate around validation that is sometimes missed is that validation studies are a limited and indirect way of demonstrating the truth of a proposition. As we have seen in the debate about the nature of progress in science, demonstrability is a key distinguishing feature of scientific knowledge. Validation is necessary to demonstrate that a result of a forensic examination can be depended upon, but it is not always enough. This is a theme to which we return.

The Issue of Contextual Bias and Confirmation Bias

Psychological bias in the forensic examiner is not a newly recognised issue. Song Ci writes about the difficulty in being set a task of re-examination of another coroner's work and that the task 'is not to verify a previous verdict, but to guard against any injustice being done' (2010, p. 14). Furthermore, forensic examiners have to put aside a variety of psychological considerations, including 'fear of offending the coroner who presided at the previous examination [… and] anxiety to suit the report to the wishes of superior officers' and so on. Instead, the task is to 'proceed with caution and justice to make the most careful examination possible … to arrive at the unvarnished truth' (p. 15). However, we now know that guarding against such fears and anxieties is not enough; no human analyst can in fact relieve themselves of their psychological biases – such biases are inevitable and need to be mitigated by designing them out of the analysis process itself.

Good reviews of the state of the art of cognitive and contextual bias in forensic science are provided by Found (2015), Stoel (2015), and Edmond (2017), and each of these set out that honest, diligent forensic scientists are subject to cognitive biases (in the same way we all are in our day-to-day decision-making). Possibly the most cited study in this context is that of Dror et al. (2006). Dror took fingerprints from real cases of expert fingerprint examiners, where half of the cases had been decided by those examiners as being individualisations (matches) and half as exclusions (not matches). These fingerprints were then presented back to the same examiner under one of two conditions – in the control condition, no contextual information was given, but in the experimental condition, the examiners were provided with a story about the origins of the print that tested whether the story would bias their judgment against their original conclusion. When presented with contextual information, the expert forensic scientists gave contradictory information from their original judgments in two thirds of the cases. This stark example has been replicated by Dror and others not only in fingerprinting, but also in other forensic sciences, including the interpretation of DNA evidence (e.g. Jeanguenat et al., 2017). Cognitive psychologists typically break these biases down into two main types – contextual bias, such as that created by Dror (2006), and confirmation bias, a particular form of contextual bias where the context is used to set up an expectation that might be confirmed.

Responses to such research are mixed across different forensic science types. The UK FSR (FSR, 2020a) provides guidance on designing bias out of the processes of forensic investigation, from the collection of forensic samples by Scene of Crime Officers (SOCOs), through to specific lab disciplines of DNA mixtures, fingerprints and generic marks, and particulate trace evidence. In every case, the focus is on mitigation strategies – for example, in fingerprint examination, it is largely unnecessary for the print examiner to be given any story of the origins of the prints under examination, and so no case story should be given to the examiner. In contrast to this mitigation advice, the PCAST (2016) report focusses on the distinction between objective and subjective methods, stating starkly that

> Objective methods are, in general, preferable to subjective methods. Analyses that depend on human judgment … are obviously more susceptible to human error, bias, and performance variability across examiners. In contrast, objective, quantified methods tend to yield greater accuracy, repeatability and reliability. (pp. 46–7)

This seems to suggest that objective sciences are not susceptible to bias, but this runs counter to the growing evidence base, such as Jeanguenat et al.'s (2017) evidence of contextual bias in DNA evidence. Also, as pointed out by the DOJ report (2021), any distinction between subjective and objective methods may in fact be at best slippery. More broadly, there has been some pushback from the forensic science community on the reliance of objective methods over human expertise so that whilst Evett et al. (2017) acknowledge the weaknesses of qualitative subjective opinions, they also argue against viewing the ideal position of the scientist as a black box:

> We do not see the future forensic scientist as an *ipse dixit* machine – whatever the opinion, we expect the scientist to be able to explain it in whatever detail is necessary for the jury to comprehend the mental processes that led to it. (p. 21)

Evett et al.'s argument here is essentially a complaint about the limitations of validation alone. As we shall see, similar concerns can be raised, even where there is strong validation, against wholly automated methods, where decision-making in individual cases can become resistant to explanation as to how the decision was reached.

Avoiding the negative consequences of cognitive biases in forensic expertise requires a recognition of where the judgements exist in apparently objective forensic analysis protocols and procedures, as well as through providing protocols to minimise those subjective judgements and creating mitigation strategies to design out the possibility of bias. Often such judgements are implicit and go unnoticed, and they require a critical eye to be brought to the fore. In the context of forensic authorship analysis, Argamon (2018) demonstrates how apparently objective, computational authorship analysis techniques in fact rely on a series of subjective, expert judgements.

The Issue of a Logically Correct Analysis

In most jurisdictions, a substantial task of the court is to decide the facts of the case – to decide *what happened*. It is in this regard that the judge(s) or jury is referred to as the trier-of-fact. As we have discussed with regard to forensic evidence, this requires a process of inference or prediction from observations to past events.

In the England and Wales Criminal Practice Directions (CrimPD, 2015), it is made explicit that it is the role of the expert witness to assist the court in decision-making, but absolutely not to determine the ultimate issue. It has, however, been a common framing of the role of the forensic expert witness in identification evidence that they should arrive at an opinion of match/non-match between a known sample and the sample collected from a crime scene. It is partly for this reason that Morrison et al. (2017) critique the PCAST (2016) report for the view that forensic examination should involve a two-stage procedure in which the first stage is 'match'/'non-match' and the second stage is empirical assessment of sensitivity (correct acceptance) and false alarm (false acceptance) rates. The difficulty is that any statement of expert identification opinion in terms of match/non-match can be seen as a usurpation of the role of the trier-of-fact. It also follows that any related expression by the expert of a percentage certainty that they attach to their match/non-match opinion only limits their appropriation of the jury's role – expression of a 90 per cent chance of a match merely limits the expert's appropriation of the jury's role to that 90 per cent.

In the UK, a reframing of the role of the expert and of the role of scientific evidence has come in part as a result of a series of miscarriages of justice that have resulted from statistical and logical errors from both experts and the lower courts. The UK House of Lords Science and Technology Committee (2019) investigated the state of forensic science and its provision and focussed in part on this issue of how scientific evidence should be presented to courts. Their witnesses on this concluded that 'the statistical aspects of forensic evidence are often either simply overlooked (because they are considered too difficult) or poorly presented by both lawyers and forensic scientists' (§164).

The House of Lords Committee recommends a shift of understanding in the role of the expert witness, which parallels the approach described in the Law Commission (2011) report. This can best be described as the two-hypothesis approach. In identification evidence, there is not one hypothesis but two hypotheses that evaluate whether disputed material can be associated with a known sample collected from the suspect. Under the two-hypothesis paradigm, it is the job of the expert witness to assess separately the probability of seeing the evidence given two possible hypotheses. Thus, in a fingerprint case, the two questions for the expert would be:

- *What is the probability of seeing this set of features in the collected finger-print if the defendant had handled the object?*
- *What is the probability of seeing this set of features in the collected finger-print if someone other than defendant had handled the object?*

Only by determining both probabilities can the expert explain to the court how the jury might weigh the fingerprint evidence against the other – potentially conflicting – evidence in the case. A simplified version of possible outcomes of the expert's work is shown in Figure 3.

In cells A and C of Figure 3, we have the 'match' condition. There is a high probability of seeing a set of features (in the fingerprint collected from the crime scene) if the fingerprint did indeed come from the defendant. This is to say the crime scene fingerprint is consistent with the defendant's known fingerprint. One danger of this approach, though, is illustrated in the difference between cell A and cell C. In cell A, the features observed are common across many other people, so the evidence carries little weight. In cell C, the observed features are rare or distinctive. In this case, the evidence has more substantial weight. This is

	High probability of seeing the features if the defendant was the source.	Low probability of seeing the features if the defendant was the source.
High probability of seeing the features if someone else was the source.	A. Evidence has little weight.	B. Evidence has substantial weight that the defendant **was not** the source.
Low probability of seeing the features if someone else was the source.	C. Evidence has substantial weight that the defendant **was** the source.	D. Evidence has little weight.

Figure 3 Evidence matrix in two-hypothesis reasoning

both intuitive and can be expressed mathematically as a likelihood ratio. The reciprocal conclusion is true for the situation represented by cell B and in the situation in cell D. With regard to cell A, although this is a match, it is a relatively meaningless match and the expert has little assistance to offer the jury.

The logic of expert evidence requires that a two-hypothesis approach is followed, but it is not absolutely necessary for this to be expressed mathematically. A mathematical expression of this approach, however, can be derived, and this referred to as a likelihood ratio. Its formulation is typically given thus:

$$\textit{weight of evidence} = \frac{\Pr(E \mid H_i)}{\Pr(E \mid H_j)}$$

In this expression, Pr stands for probability and the vertical line | is read as 'given'. E is the observed evidence and H_i is the identification hypothesis. The top line of the equation can then be read as the probability of the evidence given that the defendant was the source of the evidence. H_j is the hypothesis that someone else was the source of the evidence, and so this line can be read as the probability of the evidence given that someone other than the defendant was the source of the evidence. Although this is a mathematical expression that can be applied where actual probabilities have been calculated, the greater importance of the approach is in the logic. This means that even if a more qualitative approach is taken, attention needs to be paid to both points of the consistency of features across the known and the disputed materials and also the distinctiveness of those features in some relevant population. Lucy (2013) provides a helpful introduction to this approach to forensic inference and statistics.

This idea – that the logically correct role for the expert is to help the trier-of-fact weigh each particular piece of evidence – enables the trier-of-fact to do their job in the wider case. It has been in fact argued that if all evidence in a case could be presented mathematically as likelihood ratios, then this approach might replace the jury altogether (Lindley, 1977). This might be considered an extreme, if logical endpoint to this kind of approach, particularly if combined with wholly automated systems for determining the weight of forensic evidence (but see Swofford and Champod, 2021, discussed later in this Element with regard to this possibility). A more realistic advantage to the likelihood ratio method could be the calculation of the cumulative weight of evidence across different forensic disciplines. Realisation of this is some way off, however, and would rely on all evidence to be evaluated by triers-of-fact as a mathematical weight.

There is some question as to whether the mathematical use of likelihood ratios with judges and lay juries is a good thing. Evidence is building that suggests that judges and juries are not well equipped for using these approaches in their decision-making. De Keijser and Elffers (2012) showed that both judges and forensic scientists themselves have a poor understanding of likelihood ratio expressions in forensic reports. This has been explored further by Martire et al. (2013, 2014) who show (with students performing as mock jurors) that change of belief occurred in line with both verbal and numerical likelihood expressions, but also that this belief change was weaker than the likelihood calculations would predict. Furthermore, they observed a 'weak evidence effect' where weak evidence of guilt tended to be interpreted as reducing the likelihood of guilt rather than increasing it marginally, and that the numerical presentation of likelihoods was more resistant to this effect.

In spite of these issues with humans' reasoning with likelihoods, it can be seen that simply declaring a match or non-match has little value in its own right, without also understanding the possibility of matches in other persons. This paradigm shift, however, has not yet properly taken hold. Bali et al. (2020) show that the categorial match/non-match statements are still in the majority across eight forensic science disciplines. The slow uptake may be partly because using the likelihood ratio can depend upon validation studies, which in turn depend on producing databases of population statistics. This may be possible and has been achieved in some areas (such as fingerprinting), but it presents difficulties where population statistics are difficult to collect or even where it is difficult to conceptually formulate a population at all. As we will see, this may be the case for forensic authorship analysis and it also may be true in other forensic disciplines.

Development in Law of Admissibility

Alongside the progress in forensic science itself has come development in law and policy. Some developments in law intend to address the aforementioned concerns with validation. This has been significantly discussed elsewhere (e.g. Grant and MacLeod, 2020; Tiersma and Solan, 2002), and most of these discussions focus on the US federal Daubert standard for the admissibility of evidence. The Daubert standard is in fact an interpretation of the application of the 1975 Federal Rule of Evidence 702 and comprises four potential criteria for judging whether expert evidence should be admitted:

- whether the theory offered has been tested;
- whether it has been subjected to peer review and publication;
- the known rate of error; and
- whether the theory is generally accepted in the scientific community.

Daubert v. Merrell Dow Pharmaceuticals, Inc. (509 U.S. 579 (1993))

The *Kumho Tire Co. v. Carmichael (119 S.Ct. 1167 (1999))* ruling of the US Supreme Court confirmed that these criteria apply to anyone claiming an expertise (not just scientists), and the case law was reflected in the revision to the Federal Rule of Evidence 702 (2000).

Just as the Daubert–Kumho criteria only provide guidance on how a court might assess the scientific credentials of evidence, so there is some commentary that the courts have recognised this flexibility and not strictly applied them. Thus, Cheng (2013) observes, 'Daubert in practice fundamentally differs from Daubert in theory' (p. 542) and suggests that 'expert testimony is given a "hard look" for intellectual rigor, but nothing more' (p. 543). He further argues that one aspiration for evidence should be that it is 'sufficiently transparent to permit reasoned decision making' (p. 547) by the trier-of-fact. As Cheng points out, such an aspiration could challenge both ad hominem subjective expertise and computational analyses, where 'researchers have little idea why [a method] works as a matter of substantive theory' (p. 548), effectively arguing against the *ipse dixit* human expert, and also that it applies against a computational or algorithmic *ipse dixit* machine.

In UK contexts, there have been similar developments in law and policy around the admissibility of scientific evidence. Grant and MacLeod (2020) show the law developed on admissibility ultimately points (via the Canadian Supreme Court) back to the Daubert standards. Following the Law Commission report on expert evidence (2011), the UK government decided not to legislate for statutory Daubert-like hearings, but issues surrounding the admissibility of expert evidence are heard in pretrial hearings and tested against common law, the Criminal Practice Directions, and, less formally, against standards developed by the FSR. Criminal Practice Directions as a form of statutory instrument can be amended without primary legislation, and since 2005, the power to make such amendments lies with the Lord Chief Justice. This power is used very frequently (forty-three times in the past nine years), and the provision on expert evidence was most significantly updated with regard to expert evidence in 2015 (and since then updated seven further times with more minor changes). Para 19A.4 citing the *R v. Dlugosz* judgment on DNA evidence states:

> It is essential to recall the principle which is applicable, namely in determining the issue of admissibility, the court must be satisfied that there is a sufficiently reliable scientific basis for the evidence to be admitted.
>
> CrimPD (2015, 19A.4)

The Directions go on to set out the obligations of the expert witness to the court and the basis on which their evidence should be admitted. At 19A.5, these are set out in detail as 'factors which the Court may take into account in determining the reliability of expert evidence and therefore admissibility'. These include a focus on validity of methods, explanation of how safe an inference is (which it suggests might be done in terms of significance testing 'or in other appropriate terms'), degree of precision of the test, and so on. It also sets out at 19.B the statement and declaration that an expert witness must make within their report and for which they can be held in contempt if they breach it. This statement begins:

> I understand that my duty is to help the court to achieve the overriding objective by giving independent assistance by way of objective, unbiased opinion on matters within my expertise, both in preparing reports and giving oral evidence. I understand that this duty overrides any obligation to the party by whom I am engaged or the person who has paid or is liable to pay me.
>
> (CrimPD 19B.1)

Expert witnesses can and have been prosecuted for contempt of court for breaching this duty. In *Liverpool Victoria Insurance Co Ltd v. Zafar* (2019), a medical expert was found guilty of contempt for submitting a false statement of truth and was initially sentenced to six months' imprisonment, suspended for two years, but his own insurers appealed the sentence as too lenient and the Court of Appeal raised the sentence to nine months to be served immediately.

A final innovation in CrimPD (2015) is that it makes provision in criminal trials for pre-hearing discussion between the expert witnesses. This process, sometimes referred to as 'hot-tubbing' experts, can be entered into by agreement of the two parties or by order of the court. In these meetings, the experts from each side are asked to discuss the case to resolve issues of dispute where this is possible, and then to write a joint report in which their issues of agreement and disagreement are set out.

Along with the Criminal Practice Directions in the UK, the FSR has a statutory duty to improve forensic science evidence, and she has also developed policy briefs and instructions to forensic science providers covering validation (FSR, 2020b) and confirmation bias (FSR, 2020a), and although these do not have legal force, they are highly influential and provide 'advice and guidance so providers of forensic science services can demonstrate compliance with common standards' (www.gov.uk/government/organisations/forensic-science-regu lator/about). In an adversarial system, this superstructure of law, statuary instruments, guidance, and codes from a regulator provides a relatively responsive framework for improving the quality of admitted evidence.

Conclusions on the Idea of Progress in Forensic Science

Since the origins of modern forensic science, there has never been such a dramatic shift as that triggered by the development of DNA profiles in the late 1980s. We have demonstrated that in each of three main areas, there is an impetus for dramatic change amounting to the paradigm shift anticipated by Saks and Koehler (2005). These issues are the validation of methods, the mitigation or elimination of contextual biases, and the development in how expert evidence should be logically presented to the courts. In many areas of forensic science, including in authorship analysis work, the potential for progress across these areas is largely unrealised and older (possibly incommensurable) practices persist. Whilst this persistence might be explained as institutional inertia or even the invested self-interest of current practitioners, this situation raises potential legal issues of whether older approaches are good enough and whether ignoring these developments might provide grounds of appeal for significant numbers of cases. But change is coming, and it has serious implications across forensic science and for forensic authorship analysis work. As the UK FSR writes:

> Courts should not have to judge whether this expert or that expert is 'better', but rather there should be a clear explanation of the scientific basis and data from which conclusions are drawn. (FSR, 2020, p. 2)

In 2004, at the time of the Barot case, neither the National Academy of Sciences report in the USA nor the Law Commission's report on expert evidence in the UK had been written and, with hindsight, it is hard to view authorship evidence in that case entirely positively. That and other cases of that time (and earlier) relied on unvalidated features and methods, analyses which had to be subject to all sorts of unnoticed biases, and on expressions of results which were logically flawed. In the next Section, we consider how the issues of validation, problems of contextual bias, and use of the dual hypothesis approach have been, are being, and indeed should be applied to forensic authorship analysis.

4 Progress in Forensic Authorship Analysis

Given the progress in forensic science over the past twenty to thirty years, the nature and practice of forensic authorship analysis requires re-evaluation. In addition to examining theoretical and practical advances, this Section addresses whether practice has been changed by the revolution in forensic science, taking each of the three issues of validation, confirmation bias, and correct forensic inferencing in turn, and it addresses how forensic authorship analysis might move forward in the context of this scientific revolution.

Progress with Regard to Approaches to Forensic Authorship Analysis

Progress in the Idea of an Author

With regard to developments of the idea of an author, it is necessary to acknowledge Eckert's (2012) identification of the three waves of variation studies in sociolinguistics. She points to the first wave as originating in Labov's (1966) study of social stratification in New York City, which examines the relationship between linguistic variables and demographic categories. The second wave integrates a more personal or local interpretation of the demographic categories in terms of meaningful speech communities. In contrast to the first two waves, the third wave focusses more on language styles, which reflect social meanings as performances. One implication of third-wave variation studies is a suggestion that individual authors might have a broad collection of resources they can draw on to perform different identities in differing contexts and with differing audiences (see e.g. Johnstone, 1996, 2009). This view is most usefully summarised by Bucholtz and Hall (2004, 2005), who suggest that linguistic identity performances are emergent from interaction. They note that every interaction positions the interactant demographically and culturally and that interactions index those identity positions through overt mentions, evaluations, and specific linguistic selections. These identities are constructed through relational comparisons and contrasts and involve footing within the interaction and orientation to the interaction.

Finally, they note that identity performance can be partially deliberate and partially habitual and thus can be less than fully conscious.

Much contemporary work in forensic authorship analysis appears to ignore these insights into the nature of identity and authorship, presupposing a given essentialist position with regard to idiolect, giving rise to an expectation that linguistic variables can simply pick out an individual. With such a framing, problems with cross-genre comparison or accommodation are reduced to issues with awkward covariates, to be designed out of authorship problems to reveal the linguistic individual, rather than recognising that these aspects of a text comprise linguistic choices and expressions of identity by that individual. There are, however, notable exceptions to the essentialist position. These include Bamman et al.'s (2014) study of gendered language on Twitter, which starts by demonstrating a standard sociolinguistic profiling approach: they use Twitter profile information to identify tweets by self-identified men and tweets by self-identified women and then identify discriminating linguistic choices and patterns which separate the two groups. Having achieved this, they go on to complicate their investigation to show that those linguistic features which pick out men also pick out those women with mostly male followers, and, conversely, that those linguistic features which pick out women also pick out men who mostly have female followers. This study elegantly demonstrates cross-gender accommodation and supports the third-wave insight that we use linguistic resources to perform gendered linguistic styles, rather than that features are direct markers of gender. It thus suggests that any attempt at author profiling needs to be limited to observations that an individual uses a style of language which might be associated with a demographic category, but that language cannot predict the sex or gender, ethnicity, or indeed membership in any essential category. Considerably more theoretical work needs to be carried out on the implications of such findings with regard to the very concept of authorship. Grant and MacLeod (2018, 2020) offer a theory of authorship in terms of resources and how these resources both enable and constrain different individual performances of identity, but significantly more discussion is required in this area if forensic authorship analysis is to proceed from a well-considered theoretical foundation.

It is not only at the theoretical level that there has been at least some recognition that authorship of texts is complex and multifaceted, and in at least one case this has been reflected in a case judgment. In 2005, HVY, a consortium of former owners of 60 per cent of the Yukos oil company, took the Russian Federation to the Permanent Court of Arbitration in The Hague. In 2014, a tribunal – comprising three arbitrators along with tribunal assistant Martin Valasek – found that the Russian Federation had illegally seized assets from Yukos, and awarded HVY US$50 billion in compensation. In 2015, Russia contested the award on several grounds at the District Court of The Hague and the decision was overturned. Russia's challenge included an authorship analysis carried out by Carole Chaski (later supported by Walter Daelemans) which concluded that Valasek had illicitly authored more than half of the sections of the awards text. HVY appealed the District Court's decision, and in February 2020, the Hague Court of Appeal reinstated the award.

Coulthard and Grant were asked to provide reports commenting on Chaski and Daelemans' evidence, and one significant critique was that their authorship analyses presupposed that each subsection of the Award text had a single author. Drawing on Love (2002), Coulthard and Grant argued that this was a particularly naïve assumption for legal judgments. Using Love's framework, they contended that no section of the awards text was likely the product of a single executive author, and thus that Chaski and Daelemans' attempts at authorship attribution were compromised from the outset. In February 2020, the Hague Court of Appeal essentially agreed with this analysis:

> The Court of Appeal considers the studies by Chaski and Daelemans to be problematic in the sense that indeed – as argued by HVY – the text of a multiple-handed judgment will not always be written by a single author and that the assumption that the other authors 'usually at most respond with a single proposal for deletion or insertion' is by no means always valid.
>
> (*HVY v. The Russian Federation* §6.6.5)

The judgment goes on to say that the Court of Appeal assumes that Valasek carried out 'drafting work' (§6.6.6), and that this did not mean that he advised the Tribunal with regard to the legal issues; it further acknowledges that 'the Yukos Awards consist to a large extent of summaries of factual and legal positions of the parties' (§6.6.9.) On this the Tribunal concludes that

> What matters in the end is that the arbitrators have decided to assume responsibility for the draft versions of Valasek, whether in whole or in part and whether or not amended by them. (§6.6.10)

In short, without using the terms *precursory* and *executive authorship*, they accepted the analysis that even if Valasek *did* write sections of the award text, this would not have been contrary to the Tribunal's mandate and would thus have been unimportant. What the Yukos case points to is that the court in this case was receptive to a critique based in a genre analysis and an analysis of the functions of authorship. Furthermore, in looking forward, it points to the need for a standard operating procedure at the outset of a case to establish the linguistic feasibility of every authorship analysis. Such a case formulation protocol is provided in what follows.

Progress in Stylometry and Stylistics

The area in which there has been the most obvious advances in authorship analysis, outside of a forensic context, is in computational approaches in stylometry. Advances in both sheer computational power and in the statistical techniques of machine learning and categorisation of texts has led to improved results and a standardisation of approaches. The iterative PAN competitions have provided a framework for testing and driving up standards and understandings of the reliability and vulnerabilities of different approaches such that Ainsworth and Juola (2018) suggest that it provides a model for other forensic sciences. There have also been improvements in the analysis of very short texts (e.g. Grieve et al., 2019) and in the numbers of candidate authors who can be considered (e.g. Kredens et al., 2019). Finally, there also has been some progress in how explicable the results can be (e.g. Argamon et al., 2013; Kestemont, 2014). All of these improvements are relevant to forensic cases. However, as noted earlier in this Element, the standardisation of computational approaches itself might be considered an obstacle to progress – there is now a typical basket of features used in most studies (alongside the n-gram approach), and with some exceptions there appears to be little progress in developing a fuller suite of higher-level pragmatic and discursive features. One response to any such complaint that higher-level features are not being developed is that the low-level features are the 'objectively identifiable features' (Ainsworth and Juola, 2018, p. 1171) and that coding language at a higher level brings with it greater human effort, which means an analyst's judgement, possible error, and, ultimately, unreliability. A counterargument to such a position might point to the many linguistic studies that run convincing reliability studies on coding higher-level features (e.g. Chiang and Grant (2017), which demonstrates reliable coding of low-level rhetorical moves in adult–child sexual abuse conversations). Advocates of stylometry, however, might also point to the success rates achieved with lower-level features, rendering any such development of higher-level features risky and pointless.

With regard to PAN more generally, it is hard to agree with Ainsworth and Juola (2018) that it provides the model for other forensic sciences. Whilst PAN competitions may provide a degree of developmental or foundational validation to authorship analysis generally, they do not do so with forensically relevant texts or problems and cannot stand in as forensic validation studies. Because they are not designed as validation studies for forensic work, there is little consideration of issues of contextual bias and the methods discussed do not address the issue of calibration to case-specific problems. Furthermore, the PAN competitions seem currently wedded to either classification models or to the match/non-match paradigm in expression of results, rather than considering the weight of evidence for dual hypotheses. All of these issues, though, are fixable, and PAN could become a useful vehicle for improvement of *forensic* authorship analysis. One step towards fixing such issues, provided by Juola (2021), at least tries to establish a protocol for two-text authorship verification tasks of blog posts, even though the other issues remain.

The successful computational authorship analysis approaches already are finding applications in intelligence work in policing and security contexts (e.g. Argamon, 2009), but they have generally fared less well in the courtroom. This is largely to do with the further issue of explicability. For example, in *PS v. LP [2013] EWCOP 1106*, Grant and MacLeod (2020) report a case of a disputed will where a heavily computational approach received negative commentary from a judge who ultimately dismissed this evidence in their deliberations. The stylometric evidence in this case seems to have fallen partly because of a lack of explicability of the outcome of the analysis. Grant and MacLeod argue that the evidence provided failed Cheng's (2013) 'hard-look test', which suggests that forensic evidence must enable the trier-of-fact to make a rational decision. A jury's rational decision-making not only depends upon logically correct reasoning, but also upon on how well the jury can understand the process by which the opinion was reached. Ultimately, this is the assertion of science as the provision of demonstrable truths and of forensic science on the idea that the demonstration of truths is possible within courtroom processes. Validation studies are necessary but not sufficient to demonstrate the worth of scientific evidence in court. Unless we are to do away with human finders of fact in the court process (as suggested by Lindley, 1977), the role of the human has to include the testing of the evidence against the defendant. Presenting a juror with an *ipse dixit* black box, however well validated, remains an insufficient demonstration if it prevents an examination of how the specific conclusion in a specific case was reached. In authorship analysis work, this demonstration requires both validation of method and explicability of outcome such that the analyst can describe the differences and similarities between authors A and B and show that the features used in the analysis are distinctive in a relevant population of texts.

Swofford and Champod (2021) consider the broader issue of computational or automated analysis of evidence in comparison with other areas of high-stakes decision-making (such as expert medical systems or driverless car systems). They suggest a series of degrees of automation can be observed, which might in some contexts be viewed as a progressive path to greater automation, but also argue for different ways in which algorithms can be implemented in a responsible and practical manner (perhaps without the objective of full automation).

Swofford and Champod propose five levels of algorithmic involvement:

No Algorithmic Involvement

Level 0.   **Algorithm Assistance**: where the human expert forms their opinion based on subjective observations, after which an algorithm *may* be used as an optional assistance tool to be considered by the examiner in the finalising of their opinion.

Level 1.   **Algorithm Quality Control**: where the human expert forms their opinion based on subjective observations, after which an algorithm *must* be used as a required quality control. The expert opinion must be supported by the algorithm output or if there is a there needs to be a standard operating procedure as to how such a conflict is adjudicated and reported.

Level 2.   **Algorithm-Informed Evaluation**: now the algorithm *must be used before* any subjective evaluation is formed. The algorithm, at least in part, forms some of the basis of the expert analysis and where there is conflict between the experts' opinions there needs to be a standard operating procedure as to how such a conflict is adjudicated and reported. Swofford and Champod write, 'The key benefit of this level is that the algorithm is implemented in a way that enables the expert to leverage the output of the algorithm as a factor when evaluating the overall value of the evidence. The key limitation to this level is that the interpretation remains dependent on subjective elements from the expert' (p. 30).

Level 3.   **Algorithm-Dominated Evaluation**: the algorithm is used as the basis for the conclusion. The human expert oversees the process to ensure it is applied appropriately.

Level 4.   **Algorithm-Only Evaluation**: the algorithm is used as the basis for the conclusion without any human evaluation or oversight.

This is an interesting framework to consider with regard to forensic authorship evidence. From the judgment in *LP [2013] EWCOP 1106*, it appears that the linguist who was criticised had gone immediately to Level 3 or 4 and was unable to offer any further evaluation or explanation that might have assisted the court. His evidence was appraised as effectively coming from an *ipse dixit* machine and rejected on that basis.

The lack of explicability in many stylometric analyses might be addressed by adopting the parallel approaches of either Level 1 or 2 where the expertise with regard to explanation of results (what Author A does that is different to Author B) is provided by a stylistic analysis, and that improved validation testing offered by the PAN competitions can be leveraged by the stylometric approach. The real difficulty within Swofford and Champod's framework would be in those cases where the human expert and the algorithm disagree. In these situations, any standard operating procedure would at least require considerable re-evaluation and explanation of the analyses. In adversarial court cases at least, the consequence would likely be that the evidence of authorship would not be offered, nor would it be admitted. A requirement for agreement between stylistic and stylometric methods might in fact be a positive result for the discipline and for the delivery of justice.

With regard to progress in stylistic analyses per se, there have certainly been more authorship cases admitted in court worldwide, and most of these cases appear to draw on the stylistic approach. It appears from anecdotal accounts and from events such as the AIFL 2021 symposium, International Approaches to Linguistic Casework, that expert evidence in these cases is indeed based in painstaking linguistic description that documents differences and similarities in textual choices between different authors. Such an approach rests on the expert's subjective expertise in linguistics, and the result is that this leaves it open to the potential challenge that it is overly subjective and unvalidated. The lack of progress is in part because practitioners tend not to publish standardised operating procedures or protocols. Grant (2013) publishes a sketched protocol which is developed a little further in Grant and Grieve (2022), but these examples do not address all aspects of the analysis. It seems obvious that the reliability of stylistic approaches to authorship analysis requires the publication of protocols, which can be critiqued and then subjected to validation studies. The validation of protocols offers a middle path between, on one hand, computational systems operating within generalised developmental validation for a range of authorship problems, and, on the other, proficiency-testing of individual experts.

Progress with regard to Validation

Forensic authorship analysis appears to have been uninterested or resistant to true validation studies. The PAN competitions currently have not been designed to function as validation studies for forensic problems, although Ainsworth and Juola (2018) provide strong claims that these competitions can function as such. As Ainsworth and Juola (2018) point out, 'the development of accuracy benchmarks through the use of shared evaluation corpora on which practitioners can test their methodologies' (p. 1176) is an important and considerable contribution. Further to this, they note that there is an important issue of a normative change in the field to expect open publication of methods and results, and therefore critique and development in stylometry are occurring in a collaborative space. For all these strengths there are two principal issues with treating the PAN competitions as validation studies in specifically forensic authorship analysis, which both amount to the observation that they are not designed as such. First, the evaluation of authorship tasks are drawn in terms of success in classification. As is typical in such designs, a blind validation set is used to test each entry. The confusion matrix of precision and recall (based on percentages of true positives, false positives, false negatives, and true negatives) is reduced to an F1 score indicating overall performance. This is useful as far as it goes in evaluating various models against one another, but as we have seen, presentation of results in a forensic context requires a different design to understand the *weight* of evidence for parallel hypotheses. It would require different evaluation designs to address this issue, but such a change would be well within the reach of future PAN competitions.

The other aspect of PAN where change would be useful is in working with forensically relevant problems and data sets. There has to date been no comprehensive survey of practitioners of forensic authorship cases, how analyses are used, and which are submitted in evidence (the closest study to aim at such a survey is perhaps Giménez et al., 2021), and there is a strong need for a well-designed assessment of end user needs in this area. From such an assessment of current cases, and also a survey of the needs of law enforcement, a better understanding could enable the building of forensically relevant data sets. In the area of forensic speech comparison, Morrison (2018) describes an automatic voice comparison case where a system was used which was not validated in case-realistic conditions. He shows that performance was markedly worse than when case-realistic conditions were used so that the performance figures reported to the court would have been inadvertently inflated and the evidence given greater weight than was empirically justified. In terms of forensically realistic textual data, we know from publication (e.g. Coulthard et al., 2017; Grant, 2013) and anecdote that at least some of the forensic authorship cases include text types such as SMS messaging, apps such as WhatsApp, and social media such as Twitter, and we further know that standard Natural Language Processing (NLP) tools for tagging and parsing are not particularly robust for such texts (e.g. Horsmann, 2018). Further to any processing issues is the simple fact that such texts are short and analyses sometimes come down to the authorship of a single message. If PAN could replicate such conditions, this would be a significant step forward. It is difficult to argue with Morrison's (2018) conclusion that 'training using data reflecting the conditions of the case and calibrating system output should be standard practice' (Morrison, 2018, p. e7).

Forensic authorship analysis is not alone as a forensic science discipline in lacking credible validation studies. Many forensic disciplines still lack validation studies and where they have occurred, they can disrupt established practices and perceptions of expertise. It is, however, untenable to ignore the need for validation and there are a number of possibilities in this regard. One issue is whether it is possible to design meaningful validation studies for authorship analysis given the sources of variation in language across genres, modes of production, and audiences, as well as the complexity in identifying the nature of the linguistic individual, and this may be where calibration has a role to play.

As early as 2001, Grant and Baker set out the basic problem in corpus construction with regard to demonstrating the general reliability of stylometric authorship markers. They raise the question of whether it is better to work with a focussed corpus, with less linguistic diversity, but where it may be harder to discriminate between authors, or better to work with a general more broadly conceived corpus:

> On one side of the dilemma, if we are attempting to demonstrate the reliability of a particular authorship method, it might be better to sample narrowly, demonstrating success in the more difficult problem, rather than attempt to find typical texts that are more representative of a wider linguistic community … The difficulty with this approach is that it undermines the possibility of generalisation and thus conclusions cannot be drawn about the general usefulness or the reliability of markers studied in this way. On the other side of the dilemma, a wide general corpus may be examined, and markers may be found which distinguish socio-linguistically disparate texts. For example, Dickens may be discriminated from Shakespeare, say, by comparing word-length distributions, but from this discovery it is difficult to conclude that such a marker of authorship will apply to a case where authors might be thought to be socio-linguistically close. (Grant and Baker, 2001, p. 70)

Grant (2007) suggests a solution to this problem through a twin approach of using a general authorship corpus to demonstrate generalised differences between markers of authorship and then a comparison corpus of relevant texts produced by candidate authors in a specific case. This suggestion is paralleled for other disciplines by the UK FSR, who refers to developmental validation and internal validation of methods used in a specific lab (FSR, 2020, §6.2.7); and, as discussed in the context of automatic speaker recognition, Morrison (2018) draws a distinction between validation to refer to population-level reliability and calibration to refer to local demonstration that the features discriminate in case-specific circumstances. This idea relates to Grant's (2010, 2020) conception of pairwise and small group distinctiveness and population-level distinctiveness. The model advocated as a solution in Morrison et al. (2021) suggests that some of the perceived issues with a computational stylometry might be resolved by taking a validation-then-calibration approach. Without a calibration step demonstrating that features discriminate between the authors in a particular case and with texts from those authors in a relevant genre, generally demonstrated stylometric methods cannot be said to be reliable in a specific instance, and should not be used.

A further issue for stylometry is the use of word or character n-gram techniques where in each case a different feature set (set of n-grams) will be used. Setting aside the issue of the linguistic interpretability of some n-grams, there is a further issue that in every case a different set of linguistic features will be generated, and it may be neither logically nor practically possible to provide validation in advance for every individual n-gram used in an analysis. In such situations, the n-gram approach is essentially used as a feature-finding protocol, and the decision-making approach (either statistical or machine learning) effectively weighs or filters the features in terms of their utility in the classification model. This might be seen as effectively carrying out a calibration exercise. Prior validation could be done of the whole n-gram system of feature finding rather than of each feature, and this seems to be a logically tenable position in truly closed-set problems. Where there is a more open set, the difficulty is that this renders the calibration stage impossible. Validation of the whole n-gram approach, treated as a black-box decision-making system, amounts to a rather indirect demonstration of the reliability of the method and may be subject to further problems like those described in Morrison (2018).

The issues with validation of n-gram approaches appear to be parallel to those of validation of stylistic approaches. Stylistics as an approach is essentially a feature-finding exercise by stylistic experts, and for small, closed sets focussing on local validation (or calibration) it may be sufficient. The alternative mentioned by Cheng (2013) and Solan (2013) is proficiency testing of experts. Proficiency testing faces the same issues as validation of black-box algorithmic systems, in that it only addresses error rates in the general case, not the ability of the expert in a particular case.

A different possibility is to run validation of protocols for stylistic authorship analyses. Each protocol would need to be fairly specific to problem types, and perhaps even text genres, but general enough to be done in advance of specific cases. For example, it would be possible to define a protocol for small, closed sets for short-form messages, and a different protocol for emails (or more generally for texts between 50 and 250 words). Such protocols could be validated across a group of stylistic experts to gain information on error rates, which might be considered and used to further improve protocols as per the PAN competitions in stylometry. Implementation of validation studies of published protocols in authorship analysis should be an important priority for research in the discipline across stylistic and stylometric approaches. Such validation studies would rest on a protocol for case formulation, as is discussed later in this Element, and could also mitigate issues of contextual bias.

Progress with regard to Contextual Bias

The development of analysis protocols is clearly also a partial solution to the issues of cognitive bias. Grant (2013) and Grant and Grieve (2022) sketch out potential ideas for protocols and ways of working that directly address the issue of contextual bias. Contextual bias in authorship analysis arises differently than in many other forensic disciplines because the textual data in authorship analyses often contain the biasing details of the case, the narrative of what has happened, and these cannot be wholly shielded from the analyst. There is no ideal solution to this which makes it more important to recognise and mitigate the biases that will be present in every analyst and in every case. It is important to recognise that contextual biases exist for stylometric as well as stylistic approaches. Argamon (2018) lists the numerous decisions required in a stylo-metric analysis, and each of these decisions provides an entry point for potential bias. It needs also to be recognised, though, that any protocol can be disrupted unless there is wholehearted commitment to the idea that the duty of the expert witness is to the court and to the science rather than to the hiring party. Approaching a case problem in this state of mind is an issue of professional integrity and has to be the foundational mitigation against bias from which all else flows.

The principle set out in Grant and Grieve (2022) is a division of labour between a case manager and a case analyst. It is the role of the case manager to liaise with the client (whether police, defence solicitor, or party in a civil case), to receive and evaluate the case data in the first instance and decide on or collect comparison corpora, and then to evaluate whether the data provided are suffi-cient to enable the case to proceed. One significant initial bias for experts is the desire to help. When presented with a brutal crime, the desire to help, the desire to be able to say linguistics can help deliver justice for the victim, can be overwhelming, and this is where a case formulation protocol can assist the case manager by addressing a series of narrowly focussed linguistic questions.

Once a decision has been made to take a case, the role of the case manager is to shield the case analyst from biasing contextual information. Minimally, the case manager must consider shielding the case analyst from which side of a case they are working on. They must provide the data to the case analyst in a carefully thought-through order. This may vary according to problem types as identified through the case formulation protocol, but in a small, closed-set case, a good protocol is to provide the K-documents from the various writers first. This is because the known texts tend to contain less case information than the Q-documents. Indeed, if there are sufficient data to allow for it, specific K-documents may be omitted to shield the case analyst from elements of the story or the background situation that led to this being a case in the first place. These can be reintroduced later to provide a form of validation within the analysis. The initial task of the case analyst is to carry out a comparative authorship analysis to produce a discriminating between-author feature list on the basis of these known texts. Stylistic or stylometric methods could be used for feature-finding, and once this stage has been completed, it is effectively locked. The list of features or the discriminative algorithm that separates the authors should not be changed after this stage. Next, if there are sufficient data, there is some possibility to carry out a formal or informal validation – thus it might be possible to ask the case analyst to determine whether previously held back K-documents can be correctly attributed. Only once all of this has been completed and fully reported to the case manager will the Q-document(s) be provided to the case analyst to complete the task. The case analyst will then elicit the discriminating feature set from the Q-documents and use these to provide a weight of evidence in favour of each of the possible authorship hypotheses.

This separation of roles requires an end to the forensic linguist expert working as sole practitioner and a shift to the idea of a forensic linguistic team or laboratory working a case. This would be a substantial shift against current practice, but Grant and Grieve (2022) demonstrate it can be done.[14]

Progress with regard to Logically Correct Reporting of Results

Currently there are very few research studies which fully take on a dual-hypothesis, likelihood-ratio approach to forensic authorship analysis. Ishihara (2011, 2017a, 2017b) provides the most significant contributions to date, basing his analysis in n-gram stylometric methods, and above all he demonstrates this can be done. It has not been reported that likelihood ratio expressions have been used in textual forensic linguistic casework. It is, however, clear that, in some cases at least, forensic linguists are moving beyond a match/non-match approach and rather weigh the evidence for dual hypotheses. This is the approach used in stylistic approaches which address conclusions in terms of consistency along with distinctiveness (e.g. Grant, 2013). This meets the criteria

---

[14] Others may also use a team approach, but if so, these are not reflected in the literature on methods of textual authorship analysis. I have now worked about twenty cases using this division of labour, working with a series of skilled linguists as case analysts. As well as mitigating contextual biases, it also provides a useful training function for those who wish to engage in casework but are new to it.

of logical correctness but does not do so using the mathematical expression of likelihood ratios. The limitation of not using likelihood ratios is that it prevents comparison both with other forensic disciplines generally and with regard to how weighty the authorship evidence might be in a specific case. Clearly for both stylistic and stylometric approaches, further progress requires that we should follow Ishihara's lead to conduct both validation studies using these frameworks and to develop casework protocols which create likelihood ratios representing the weight of evidence in individual cases.

5 Future Directions in Forensic Authorship Analysis

From the foregoing discussion, it seems that a true forensic science of authorship analysis is in our grasp, but also that there is considerable work to be done. As has clearly been identified, one area in which forensic authorship analysis can and indeed should progress is through the development of protocols. In Grant (2013), a high-level, five-part protocol is proposed for stylistic analysis in classification problems. The parts are:

1. Try to know as little as possible about the wider details of the case.
2. Describe the features of the known texts first.
3. The contrastive analysis should elicit consistent and distinctive features within the known texts, focussing on within-author consistency and between-author distinctiveness.
4. Carry out an examination of the query texts for the identified features.
5. Draw conclusions based on the consistency and distinctiveness of the query texts with each set of texts of known authorship.

This protocol is clearly directed towards addressing issues of confirmation bias and, as discussed in Grant and Grieve (2022), it is demonstrated how this can be strengthened by splitting the roles of case manager and case analyst. Much more work on a whole series of protocols is required – not only a different protocol to address all the authorship analysis tasks described in the taxonomy of Figure 2, but also to tackle the different genres common to forensic problems. Prior to development of these protocols, however, is the requirement for a protocol to decide whether a case is viable for *any* kind of authorship analysis – this would amount to a case formulation protocol.

The project of validation in forensic authorship analysis therefore minimally needs:

• An end-user needs analysis: a comprehensive survey of authorship analysis practitioners and those who commission them to better understand the structures of problems and cases that are either most frequent or most important to address.

- The development of a case formulation protocol: this would enable a case manager to more rigorously understand the structure of a case and to evaluate whether the case should be taken. It is only on the basis of such a formulation that specific case protocols can be developed.
- The development of a library of case protocols: these will need to elicit and address every point of decision in an analysis, including feature selection or elicitation, methods of decision-making, and expression of results. All protocols need to mitigate contextual biases.
- Validation of case protocols: a validation study then is required for each protocol and should of course include specific criteria of what sort of authorship problems it applies to, and what genre of text it has been validated with. Furthermore, these validation study designs should enable logically correct reporting of results.

A Case Formulation Protocol

A starting point is a case formulation protocol, an attempt at which is provided here. As currently conceived, this comprises a set of questions and issues for a case manager to consider before agreeing to take a case. Deciding these questions relies on the case manager's expertise in eliciting and understanding information from the client, but they keep this information from the case analyst.

These are:

1. *Consideration of the structure of the problem*
   a. *Does the problem truly have a closed set of candidate authors?*
   b. *Who is responsible for providing evidence that this is a closed-set problem?*
   c. *Is it reasonable to treat the case as a closed-set problem?*
   d. *If the problem involves an open set, how will this limit any conclusions?*

2. *Description of the query text(s)*
   This requires a description of objective features such as length and number of texts and a structured analysis to consider wider characteristics of the texts' interactional and socially situated context. This can be achieved using Hymes' (1974) SPEAKING mnemonic, which evaluates Setting, Participants, Ends, Acts Sequence, Key, Instrumentalities, Norms, and Genre. Then the genre analysis can be addressed by describing the purpose, topic, and mode of production of the text. Such an analysis can easily be institutionalised into an assessment form or similar. Once a general understanding of text types and genre has been thought through, more specific questions include:

Are there reasonable grounds to consider the query text(s) has a single author?

Does the length of a query text suggest or exclude a particular type of analysis?

3. *Description of the comparison text(s) for each candidate author*
   a. *Are there genre differences between K-documents, or between K- and Q-documents which might confound the analysis?*
   b. *Are there audience or broader contextual issues that might confound the analysis?*
   c. *Is there enough comparison material for each candidate author?*

All of the answers to these questions lead to a decision of whether a case is viable or should be declined, and also what methods might best be applied to a case whether this is a stylometric approach, a stylistic approach, or some twin-track approach making use of both techniques as advocated by Swofford and Champod (2021).

A full case formulation approach might then trigger a selection from a library of case protocols. Each of these specific protocols would have to detail the decision-making process for each approach or method, validation results for that protocol, and what calibration might be required. With regard to validation, it is these protocols which would be validated, not specific features, computer systems, or individuals' proficiencies. Such a programme would be a significant leap forward, possibly a revolution, for forensic authorship analysis.

Conclusions

Since 2004 when I received the call for help in the Dhiren Barot case, we have gained much *knowledge about* forensic science biases, validation, and statistical inference. We also know more about authors, texts, and the processes of authorship analysis itself. There has been progress in forensic authorship analysis, but we have not yet adopted the learning from the paradigm shift, the scientific revolution, in forensic science more generally. This should clearly be our next objective.

If I received the call about the Barot case today, would I behave differently? I would certainly be just as excited to be called and feel similarly pressured. I would want to help, but I would now recognise that this desire to help is itself a biasing factor. Today, at that first phone call, I would either draw up a formal case formulation or at the very least carry out a rapid assessment through asking questions about both the known and the queried texts to establish whether the case was viable and whether more texts were required. I now try to do this in each case in which I'm asked to engage. I would structure the team I gathered deliberately and differently according to an analysis plan. If we had to work on police premises through the night, I would consider how this situation might compromise and bias the analysis and how I might mitigate this. Perhaps I would split the team in two, with one team analysing and eliciting features from the known materials, and a second team analysing the *Gas Limo Project* itself. I would consider the possibility of a computational approach – there was plenty of material, but this would have required typing up the documents, inevitably introducing transcription errors. In structure, the Barot case was a verification task, an open-set problem. How could I validate the stylistic features that stood out and seemed so salient? I might consider whether this might be done post hoc by recruiting yet more analysts to determine whether the features we elicited were indeed rare in some relevant population of writing. I would also carefully consider implementing a dual-hypothesis design. All of this would certainly improve the robustness of the analysis.

But still, if I carried out the analysis today, I would not be able to draw on protocols that had been validated, or methods or systems that had been validated and calibrated on forensically relevant texts. The unusual nature of the Barot texts in fact points to the problematic nature of generalised validation of authorship analysis. Furthermore, I would not be able to point to many authorship analysis studies that explored the weight of authorship evidence in a broader forensic science context, nor for a validation study would I be able to express the result in terms of a likelihood ratio. Filling in these gaps requires much more foundational research.

Dhiren Barot, faced with the case against him, pleaded guilty to the terrorism charges and initially received forty years in prison, reduced to thirty years on appeal. Further evidence, both that which was prepared for his trial and that which has arisen subsequently, seems to support his guilty plea. Barot, however, had been charged on the basis of the linguistic evidence alone. In the UK, introduction of new evidence after formal charges have been laid requires specific permission from a judge and is not always granted. Before Barot pleaded guilty, there were significant legal arguments as to the admissibility of the linguistic evidence and to the admissibility of new evidence after the charge. Barot's guilty plea came between the hearing that admitted the linguistic evidence and the main trial, and because of this the linguistic evidence in the case was never tested in court.

If I received the Barot phone call today, I would have more robust evidence, and I hope to continue to further the research that will provide still more robust evidence as we progress. I've revisited the analysis we produced and I've thought about the non-ideal circumstance of the case. In reviewing the materials, I do believe that we found a strong weight of evidence that Barot wrote the

Gas Limo Project. I'm wholly aware that this opinion may simply be my persistent bias. Although I believe strongly that I could do a better job today, I now have a new anxiety. This is that if I was approached today under similar circumstances, I would simply decline the case: that because the circumstances and the texts would make the case appear too uncertain or even impossible, I would decide that it was undoable. To the extent that forensic linguistics is an attempt to improve the delivery of justice, it requires rigorous analysis, but it also requires engagement. There will always be a tension between current capability – *How well can I do on this case now? How much better could I do with a further twenty years of research?* – and the desire and need to engage – *Is it better to openly offer an imperfect contribution? Or should I decline the case?* The only route available is to improve the delivery of justice where we can and at the same time to make more progress in the research and practice of forensic authorship analysis.

References

Ainsworth, J., & Juola, P. (2018). Who wrote this: Modern forensic authorship analysis as a model for valid forensic science. *Washington University Law Review, 96*, 1161–89.

Argamon, S. (2009). *Computational Methods for Counterterrorism*. Springer.

Argamon, S. (2018). Computational forensic authorship analysis: Promises and pitfalls. *Language and Law/Linguagem e Direito, 5*(2), 7–37.

Argamon, S., & Koppel, M. (2013). A systemic functional approach to auto-mated authorship analysis. *Journal of Law and Policy, 21*, 299–315.

Bailey, R. (1979). Authorship attribution in a forensic setting. In D. E. Ager, F. E. Knowles, & J. Smith (eds.), *Advances in Computer-Aided Literary and Linguistic Research: Proceedings of the Fifth International Symposium on Computers in Literary and Linguistic Computing 1978 Conference* (pp. 1–15). Department of Modern Languages, University of Aston in Birmingham.

Bali, A. S., Edmond, G., Ballantyne, K. N., Kemp, R. I., & Martire, K. A. (2020). Communicating forensic science opinion: An examination of expert reporting practices. *Science & Justice, 60*(3), 216–24.

Bamman, D., Eisenstein, J., & Schnoebelen, T. (2014). Gender identity and lexical variation in social media. *Journal of Sociolinguistics, 18*(2), 135–60.

Bloch, B. (1948). A set of postulates for phonemic analysis. *Language, 24*(1), 3–46.

Bucholtz, M., & Hall, K. (2004). Language and identity. In A. Duranti, (ed.), *A Companion to Linguistic Anthropology* (pp. 369–94). Wiley.

Bucholtz, M., & Hall, K. (2005). Identity and interaction: A sociocultural linguistic approach. *Discourse Studies, 7*(4), 585–614.

Canter, D. (1992) An evaluation of the 'Cusum' stylistic analysis of confes-sions. *Expert Evidence, 1*(3), 93–9.

Cheng, E. K. (2013). Being pragmatic about forensic linguistics. *Journal of Law & Policy, 21*, 541–50.

Chiang, E., & Grant, T. (2017). Online grooming moves and strategies. *Language and Law / Linguagem e Direito, 4*(1), 103–41.

Coulthard, M. (1994). On the use of corpora in the analysis of forensic texts. *International Journal of Speech Language and the Law, 1*(1), 27–43.

Coulthard, M. (2004). Author identification, idiolect, and linguistic uniqueness. *Applied Linguistics, 25*(4), 431–47.

Coulthard, M., Johnson, A., & Wright, D. (2017). *An Introduction to Forensic Linguistics: Language in Evidence*. Routledge.

CrimPD: Criminal Practice Directions (2015) https://www.judiciary.uk/wp-content/uploads/2015/09/crim-pd-2015.pdf (Last accessed 27 February 2022)

de Haan, P., & Schils, E. (1993) Characteristics of sentence length in running text. *Literary and Linguistic Computing, 8*(1), 20–6.

de Keijser, J., & Elffers, H. (2012). Understanding of forensic expert reports by judges, defense lawyers and forensic professionals. *Psychology, Crime & Law, 18*(2), 191–207.

Dror, I. E., Charlton, D., & Péron, A. E. (2006). Contextual information renders experts vulnerable to making erroneous identifications. *Forensic Science International, 156*(1), 74–8.

Eckert, P. (2012). Three waves of variation study: The emergence of meaning in the study of variation. *Annual Review of Anthropology, 41*, 87–100.

Edmond G., Towler A., Growns B., et al. (2017). Thinking forensics: Cognitive science for forensic practitioners. *Science & Justice, 57*, 144–54. http://dx.doi.org/10.1016/j.scijus.2016.11.005

Ehrhardt, S. (2007). Forensic linguistics at the German Bundeskriminalamt. In G. Grewendorf & M. Rathert (eds.), *Formal Linguistics and Law.* Mouton de Gruyter.

England and Wales Forensic Science Regulator (FSR) (2020). *Annual Report: 17 November 2018–16 November 2019.* www.gov.uk/government/publications/forensic-science-regulator-annual-report-2019

England and Wales Forensic Science Regulator (FSR) (2020a). *Cognitive Bias Effects Relevant to Forensic Science Examinations* FSR-G-217 Issue 2. https://assets.publishing.service.gov.uk/government/uploads/system/uploads/attachment_data/file/914259/217_FSR-G-217_Cognitive_bias_appendix_Issue_2.pdf

England and Wales Forensic Science Regulator (FSR) (2020b). *Forensic Science Regulator Guidance: Validation* FSR-G-201 Issue 2. https://assets.publishing.service.gov.uk/government/uploads/system/uploads/attachment_data/file/920449/201_-_FSR-G-201_Validation_Guidance_Issue_2.pdf

Evans, C. (1998). *The Casebook of Forensic Detection: How Science Solved 100 of the World's Most Baffling Crimes.* Wiley.

Evett, I. W., Berger, C. E. H., Buckleton, J. S., Champod, C., & Jackson, G. (2017). Finding the way forward for forensic science in the US: A commentary on the PCAST report. *Forensic Science International, 278*, 16–23.

Farringdon, J. M. (1996). *Analysing for Authorship: A Guide to the Cusum Technique.* University of Wales Press.

Finegan, E. (1990). Variation in linguists' analyses of author identification. *American Speech, 65*(4), 334–40.

Finegan, E. (2021, 13–15 September). *Bit Parts in Complex Litigation: Experts Need to Follow Up International Association of Forensic Linguists Bienniel Conference*, Aston University, UK.

Fitzgerald, J. R. (2017). *A Journey to the Center of the Mind Book III*. Infinity.

Foster, D. (2000). *Author Unknown: On the Trail of Anonymous*. Macmillan.

Found, B. (2015). Deciphering the human condition: The rise of cognitive forensics. *Australian Journal of Forensic Sciences, 47*, 386–401. http://dx .doi.org/10.1080/00450618.2014.965204

Giménez, R., Elstein, S., & Queralt, S. (2021). The pandemic and the forensic linguistics caseworker's wellbeing: Effects and recommendations. *International Journal of Speech Language and the Law, 27*(2), 233–54. https://doi.org/10.1558/ijsll.19548

Grant, T. (1992). An evaluation of the Cusum analysis of the distribution of two and three letter words in a text as a forensic test of authorship [Unpublished MSc dissertation]. University of Birmingham, UK.

Grant, T. (2007). Quantifying evidence in forensic authorship analysis. *International Journal of Speech, Language & the Law, 14*(1), 1–25.

Grant, T. (2008). Approaching questions in forensic authorship analysis. In J. Gibbons & M. T. Turell (eds.), *Dimensions of Forensic Linguistics* (pp. 215–99). John Benjamins.

Grant, T. (2010). Txt 4n6: Idiolect free authorship analysis? In M. Coulthard and A. Johnson (eds.), *The Routledge Handbook of Forensic Linguistics* (pp. 508–22). Routledge.

Grant, T. (2013). Txt 4N6: Method, consistency and distinctiveness in the analysis of SMS text messages. *Journal of Law and Policy, 21*(2), 467–94.

Grant, T. (2020). Txt 4n6 revisited: Idiolect free authorship analysis? In M. Coulthard, A. May, & R. Sousa Silva (eds.), *The Routledge Handbook of Forensic Linguistics* (2nd ed.) (pp. 558–75). Routledge.

Grant, T., & Baker, K. (2001). Identifying reliable, valid markers of authorship: A response to Chaski. *Forensic Linguistics, 8*, 66–79.

Grant, T., & Grieve, J. W. (2022). The Starbuck case: Methods for addressing confirmation bias in forensic authorship analysis. In I. Picornell, R. Perkins, & M. Coulthard (eds.), *Methods in Forensic Linguistic Case Work*. Wiley.

Grant, T., & MacLeod, N. (2018). Resources and constraints in linguistic identity performance: A theory of authorship. *Language and Law/ Linguagem e Direito, 5*(1), 80–96.

Grant, T., & MacLeod, N. (2020). *Language and Online Identities: The Undercover Policing of Internet Sexual Crime*. Cambridge University Press.

Grieve, J. (2007). Quantitative authorship attribution: An evaluation of techniques. *Literary and Linguistic Computing, 22*, 251–70.

Grieve, J., Clarke, I., Chiang, E., et al. (2019). Attributing the Bixby Letter using n-gram tracing. *Digital Scholarship in the Humanities*, *34*(3), 493–512.

Hardcastle, R. A. (1993). Forensic linguistics: An assessment of the CUSUM method for the determination of authorship. *Journal of the Forensic Science Society*, *33*(2), 95–106.

Harman, G. (1965). The inference to the best explanation. *The Philosophical Review*, *74*(1), 88–95. doi:10.2307/2183532

Herring, S. C. (2004). Computer-mediated discourse analysis: An approach to researching online behavior. In S. Barab, R. Kling, & J. Gray (eds.), *Designing for Virtual Communities in the Service of Learning* (pp. 338–76). Cambridge University Press.

Hilton, M. L., & Holmes, D. I. (1993). An assessment of cumulative sum charts for authorship attribution. *Literary and Linguistic Computing*, *8*(2), 73–80.

Hitt, J. (2012, 23 July). Words on trial: Can linguists solve crimes that stump the police? *New Yorker*. www.newyorker.com/magazine/2012/07/23/words-on-trial

Hockett, C. F. (1958). *A Course in Modern Linguistics*. Macmillan.

Hollinger, D. A. (1973). TS Kuhn's theory of science and its implications for history. *The American Historical Review*, *78*(2), 370–93.

Holmes, D. I., & Tweedie, F. J. (1995). Forensic stylometry: A review of the cusum controversy. *Revue Informatique et Statistique dans les Sciences Humaines*, *31*(1), 19–47.

Horsmann, T. (2018). Robust part-of-speech tagging of social media text. Doctoral Dissertation. University of Duisburg-Essen. https://duepublico2.uni-due.de/servlets/MCRFileNodeServlet/duepublico_derivate_00045328/Diss_Horsmann.pdf

House of Lords: House of Lords Science and Technology Select Committee (2019). *Forensic Science and the Criminal Justice System: A Blueprint for Change*. https://publications.parliament.uk/pa/ld201719/ldselect/ldsctech/333/33302.htm

Hutton, W. (1782). *History of Birmingham*. Project Gutenberg. www.gutenberg.org/files/13926/13926-8.txt

Hymes, D. (1974). *Foundations in Sociolinguistics: An Ethnographic Approach*. University of Pennsylvania Press.

Ishihara, S. (2011). A forensic authorship classification in SMS messages: A likelihood ratio based approach using n-grams. In D. Molla & D. Martinez (eds.), *Proceedings of the Australasian Language Technology Association Workshop 2011* (pp. 47–56).

Ishihara, S. (2017a). Strength of forensic text comparison evidence from stylometric features: A multivariate likelihood ratio-based analysis. *The International Journal of Speech, Language and the Law, 24*(1), 67–98.

Ishihara, S. (2017b). Strength of linguistic text evidence: A fused forensic text comparison system, *Forensic Science International, 278*, 184–97.

Jeanguenat, A. M., Budowle, B., & Dror, I. E. (2017). Strengthening forensic DNA decision making through a better understanding of the influence of cognitive bias. *Science & Justice, 57*(6), 415–20.

Johnstone, B. (1996). *The Linguistic Individual: Self-Expression in Language and Linguistics*. Oxford University Press.

Johnstone, B. (2009). Stance, style and the linguistic individual. In A. Jaffe (ed.), *Sociolinguistic Perspectives on Stance*. Oxford University Press.

Juola, P. (2021). Verifying authorship for forensic purposes: A computational protocol and its validation. *Forensic Science International, 325*. https://doi .org/10.1016/j.forsciint.2021.110824

Juola, P., & Vescovi, D. (2011). Analyzing stylometric approaches to author obfuscation. In G.L. Peterson & S. Shenoi (eds.), *IFIP International Conference on Digital Forensics* (pp. 115–25). Springer.

Kaczynski, T. J. (1995). Industrial society and its future. *Washington Post* www .washingtonpost.com/wp-srv/national/longterm/unabomber/manifesto.text.htm (Last accessed 19 October 2021).

Kaye, T. (1991). Unsafe and unsatisfactory? The report of the independent inquiry into the working practices of the West Midlands Serious Crime Squad. Civil Liberties Trust.

Kestemont, M. (2014). Function words in authorship attribution: From black magic to theory? In A. Feldman, A. Kazantseva & S. Szpakowicz (eds.), *Proceedings of the 3rd Workshop on Computational Linguistics for Literature (CLfL) at EACL 2014* (pp. 59–66). Gothenburg, Sweden, 27 April 2014.

Kestemont, M., Luyckx, K., Daelemans, W., & Crombez, T. (2012). Cross-genre authorship verification using unmasking. *English Studies, 93*(3), 340–56.

Kniffka, H. (1981). *Der Linguist als Gutachter bei Gericht: Überlegungen und Materialien zu einer Angewandten Soziolinguistik*. Bouvier.

Kniffka, H. (1990). *Texte zu Theorie und Praxis forensischer Linguistik*. Walter de Gruyter.

Kniffka, H. (1996). *Recent Developments in Forensic Linguistics*. Peter Lang.

Kniffka, H. (2007). *Working in Language and Law*. Palgrave Macmillan.

Koppel, M., Akiva, N., & Dagan, I. (2006a). Feature instability as a criterion for selecting potential style markers. *Journal of the American Society for Information Science and Technology, 57*(11), 1519–25.

Koppel, M., Schler, J., & Argamon, S. (2011). Authorship attribution in the wild. *Language Resources and Evaluation, 45*(1), 83–94.

Koppel, M., Schler, J., Argamon, S. & Messeri, E. (2006b). Authorship attribution with thousands of candidate authors. In *Proceedings of the 29th Annual International ACM SIGIR Conference on Research and Development in Information Retrieval* (pp. 659–60). Association for Computing Machinery.

Kredens, K., Perkins, R., & Grant, T. (2019a). Developing a framework for the explanation of interlingual features for native and other language influence detection. *Language and Law/Linguagem e Direito, 6*(2), 10–23.

Kredens, K., Pezik, P., Rogers, L., Shiu, S. (2019b). Toward linguistic explanation of idiolectal variation: Understanding the black box. Conference presentation. IAFL 2019 Conference Melbourne, Australia.

Kuhn, T. S. (1962). *The Structure of Scientific Revolutions*. University of Chicago Press.

Labov, W. (1966). *The Social Stratification of English in New York City*. Washington, DC: Center for Applied Linguistics.

Larner, S. (2014). A preliminary investigation into the use of fixed formulaic sequences as a marker of authorship. *International Journal of Speech Language and the Law, 21*(1), 1–22.

Law Commission (2011). Expert evidence in criminal proceedings. www .lawcom.gov.uk/project/expert-evidence-in-criminal-proceedings (last accessed 19 October 2021).

Lindley, D. V. (1977). Probability and the law. *Journal of the Royal Statistical Society. Series D (The Statistician), 26*(3), 203–20. www.jstor.org/stable/ 2987898

Litvinova, T., Seredin, P., Litvinova, O., Dankova, T., & Zagorovskaya, O. (2018, September). On the stability of some idiolectal features. In A. Karpov, O. Jokisch & R. Potapova (eds.), *International Conference on Speech and Computer* (pp. 331–6). Springer.

Locard, E. (1920). *L'enquête criminelle et les méthodes scientifiques*. Flammarion.

Love, H. (2002). *Attributing Authorship: An Introduction*. Cambridge University Press.

Lucy, D. (2013). *Introduction to Statistics for Forensic Scientists*. Wiley.

Martire, K. A., Kemp, R. I., Sayle, M., & Newell, B. R. (2014). On the interpretation of likelihood ratios in forensic science evidence: Presentation formats and the weak evidence effect. *Forensic Science International, 240*, 61–8.

Martire, K. A., Kemp, R. I., Watkins, I., Sayle, M. A., & Newell, B. R. (2013). The expression and interpretation of uncertain forensic science evidence:

Verbal equivalence, evidence strength, and the weak evidence effect. *Law and Human Behavior, 37*(3), 197.

McMenamin, G. R. (1993). *Forensic Stylistics*. Elsevier.

McMenmain, G. R. (2002). *Forensic Linguistics: Advances in Forensic Stylistics*. Routledge.

Morrison, G. S. (2018). The impact in forensic voice comparison of lack of calibration and of mismatched conditions between the known-speaker recording and the relevant-population sample recordings, *Forensic Science International, 283*, e1–e7. http://dx.doi.org/10.1016/j.forsciint.2017.12.024

Morrison, G. S., Enzinger E., Hughes V., et al. (2021). Consensus on validation of forensic voice comparison. *Science & Justice, 61*(3), 299–309.

Morrison, G. S., Kaye, D. H., Balding, D. J., et al. (2017). A comment on the PCAST report: Skip the 'match'/'non-match' stage. *Forensic Science International, 272*, e7–e9. http://dx.doi.org/10.1016/j.forsciint.2016.10.018

Morton, A. Q. (1991). *Proper Words in Proper Places: A General Introduction to the Use of Cumulative Sum Techniques for Identifying the Source of Written or Spoken Utterance*. Department of Computing Science, University of Glasgow.

Mosteller, F., & Wallace, D. L. (1964). *Inference and Disputed Authorship: The Federalist*. Addison-Wesley

Mosteller, F., & Wallace, D. L. (1989). Deciding authorship. In Judith Tanur et al. (eds.), *Encyclopedia of Statistical Sciences* (pp. 115–31) Wiley.

Narayanan, A., Paskov, H., Gong, N. Z., et al. (2012, May). On the feasibility of internet-scale author identification. In *2012 IEEE Symposium on Security and Privacy* (pp. 300–14). Institute of Electrical and Electronics Engineers.

NAS: National Research Council of the [United States] National Academy of Sciences' Committee on Identifying the Needs of the Forensic Sciences Community (2009). Strengthening forensic science in the United States: A path forward. www.ncjrs.gov/pdffiles1/nij/grants/228091.pdf

Nathan, C. (2017). Liability to deception and manipulation: The ethics of undercover policing. *Journal of Applied Philosophy, 34*(3), 370–88.

Newton, R. G. (1997). *The Truth of Science: Physical Theories and Reality*. Harvard University Press.

Nini, A. (2015). *Authorship profiling in a forensic context*. PHD thesis. Aston University.

Nini, A., & Grant, T. (2013). Bridging the gap between stylistic and cognitive approaches to authorship analysis using systemic functional linguistics and multidimensional analysis. *International Journal of Speech, Language & the Law, 20*(2), 173–202.

Nisbet, R. (1979). The idea of progress: A bibliographic essay. https://oll .libertyfund.org/pages/idea-of-progress-a-bibliographical-essay-by-robert-nisbet

Nisbet, R. (2009). *History of the Idea of Progress*. 2nd ed. Transaction.

PCAST: President's Council of Advisors on Science and Technology (2016). Forensic science in criminal courts: Ensuring scientific validity of feature-comparison methods. https://obamawhitehouse.archives.gov/sites/default/ files/microsites/ostp/PCAST/pcast_forensic_science_report_final.pdf

Ross, D., Jr. (1977). The sue of word-class distribution data for stylistics: Keats sonnets and chicken soup. *Poetics*, *6*, 169–95.

Ruder, S., Ghaffari, P., & Breslin, J. G. (2016). Character-level and multi-channel convolutional neural networks for large-scale authorship attribution. arXiv preprint arXiv:1609.06686.

Saks, M. J., & Koehler, J. J. (2005). The coming paradigm shift in forensic identification science. *Science*, *309*(5736), 892–5.

Sanford, A. I., Aked, J. F., Moxey, L. M., & Mullin, J. (1994). A critical cxamination of assumptions underlying the cusum technique of forensic linguistics. *Forensic Linguistics*, *1*(2), 151–67.

Sankey, H. (2018). *Rationality, Relativism and Incommensurability*. Routledge.

Searle, J. R. (1975). A taxonomy of illocutionary acts. *Language, Mind and Knowledge: Minnesota Studies in the Philosophy of Science*. 344–69.

Siegel, H. (1987). Kuhn and relativism: Is he or isn't he? In *Relativism Refuted* (pp. 47–69). Springer.

Solan, L. M. (2013). Intuition versus algorithm: The case of forensic authorship attribution. *JL & Pol'y*, *21*, 551.

Song, C. (2010). *The Washing Away of Wrongs: Collected Cases of Injustice Rectified* (original work published 1247) [2010 edition H. A. Giles, translator; M. C. Hall, editor) Lulu Press].

Stamatatos, E. (2009). A survey of modern authorship attribution methods. *Journal of the American Society for information Science and Technology*, *60*(3), 538–56.

Stoel, R. D., Berger, C. E. H., Kerkhoff, W., Mattijssen, E. J. A. T., & Dror, E. I. (2015). Minimizing contextual bias in forensic casework. In K. J. Strom & M. J. Hickman (eds.), *Forensic Science and the Administration of Justice: Critical Issues and Directions* (pp. 67–86). Sage. http://dx.doi.org/10.4135 /9781483368740.n5

Svartvik, J. (1968). *The Evans Statements: A Case for Forensic Linguistics*. University of Goteburg.

Swofford, H., & Champod, C. (2021). Implementation of algorithms in pattern & impression evidence: A responsible and practical roadmap. *Forensic*

Science International: Synergy, 3, 100142. https://doi.org/10.1016/j.fsisyn .2021.100142

Theóphilo, A., Pereira, L. A., & Rocha, A. (2019). A needle in a haystack? Harnessing onomatopoeia and user-specific stylometrics for authorship attribution of micro-messages. In *ICASSP 2019–2019 IEEE International Conference on Acoustics, Speech and Signal Processing (ICASSP)* (pp. 2692–6). IEEE.

Thompson, W., Black, J., Jain, A., & Kadane, J. (2017). *Forensic Science Assessments: A Quality and Gap Analysis–Latent Fingerprint Examination.* American Association for the Advancement of Science.

Tiersma, P., & Solan, L. M. (2002). The linguist on the witness stand: Forensic linguistics in American courts. *Language,* 78, 221–239.

United States Department of Justice (DOJ) (2021). United States Department of Justice statement on the PCAST Report: Forensic science in criminal courts: Ensuring scientific validity of feature-comparison methods. www.justice.gov /olp/page/file/1352496/download

Wenger, E., McDermott, R., & Snyder, W. M. (2002). *Cultivating Communities of Practice: A Guide to Managing Knowledge.* Harvard Business Review Press.

Whittle, H., Hamilton-Giachritsis, C., Beech, A., & Collings, G. (2013). A review of online grooming: Characteristics and concerns. *Aggression and Violent Behavior, 18*(1), 62–70.

Woodhams, J., Hollin, C. R., & Bull, R. (2007). The psychology of linking crimes: A review of the evidence. *Legal and Criminological Psychology, 12*(2), 233–49.

Wright, D. (2013). Stylistic variation within genre conventions in the Enron email corpus: Developing a text sensitive methodology for authorship research. *International Journal of Speech, Language & the Law, 20*(1).

Wright, D. (2017). Using word n-grams to identify authors and idiolects: A corpus approach to a forensic linguistic problem. *International Journal of Corpus Linguistics, 22*(2), 212–41.

Legal Cases

UK Cases

R. v. Turner [1975] Law Reports, Queen's Bench (Court of Appeal), 834–43

R. v. Hodgson appeal [2009] EWCA Crim 742

R. v. Dlugosz [2013] EWCA Crim 2

Young v. Her Majesty's Advocate [2013] HCJAC 145
Criminal Practice Directions [2015] EWCA Crim 1567
Liverpool Victoria Insurance Co Ltd v. Zafar [2019] EWCA Civ 392
Federal Rules of Evidence 702

US Cases

Daubert v. Merrell Dow Pharmaceuticals, Inc. (509 U.S. 579 (1993))
Kumho Tire Co. v. Carmichael (119 S.Ct. 1167 (1999))
Dale Brisco v. VFE corporation Superior Court of Fresno County, California, 1984
Brisco v. VFE Corp, and Related Cross-Action, 272028–2, Superior Court of Fresno County, California, 1984

The Hague Court of Appeal

HVY v. The Russian Federation [2020] – Hulley Enterprises Limited (Cyprus), Veteran Petroleum Limited (Cyprus), Yukos Universal Limited (Isle of Man) v. The Russian Federation [2020] The Hague Court of Appeal Case No. ECLI:NL: GHDHA:2020:234, Judgment dated 18 February 2020. All direct quotes from the Court of Appeal decision are taken from the unofficial English translation available at https://jusmundi.com/en/document/decision/en-yukos-universal-limited-isle-of-man-v-the-russian-federation-judgment-of-the-hague-court-of-appeal-tuesday-18th-february-2020#decision_6812 (Last accessed 27 February 2022).

Acknowledgements

This Element is the result of many conversations about forensic authorship analysis with the students and staff at Aston University and from other universities. It is also the result of many conversations with police investigators and defence solicitors about the capabilities and limitations of forensic authorship analysis. I have tried to listen and learn from all of these conversations, and they have all informed my views and improved my thinking in this area.

Specific Sections of this Element have benefitted from information, case reports, and critiques from Malcolm Coulthard, Ed Finegan, and Jerry McMenamin. I've had useful and interesting discussions with Geoff Morrison on the recent advances in forensic science, and my approach to authorship work has benefitted from valued discussions with Tammy Gales, editor of this volume and co-editor of this Elements series. I would also like to thank the anonymous reviewers who all helped improve this text. As when receiving any anonymous reviews in our field, I tried hard to not figure out who you are, but I think I failed in this endeavour – never fear; your secret identities are safe with me. With all of this help I remain of course wholly responsible for the content of this text.

I'd like to offer more general, but no less important recognition and thanks to the co-founders of the Centre for Forensic Linguistics at Aston University – my mentor and friend Malcolm Coulthard, with whom I've been discussing forensic linguistics for more than thirty years, and my colleague and friend Krzysztof Kredens, with whom I've argued about authorship and idiolect over a period of nearly fifteen years, and from whom I've learnt much through many enjoyable and valuable disagreements.

Further thanks go to John Pollard, to whom this volume is dedicated. In 2008, John joined the Centre for Forensic Linguistics as its first administrative assistant, and in 2019, he became the operations manager of the newly formed Aston Institute for Forensic Linguistics. John has since moved forward to a new role, taking with him his clearsighted vision, his considerable organisational skills, and his dogged efficiency in simply getting things done. Without John, and without his professional colleagues both at Aston and at universities around the world, none of this would have happened.

I thank you all.

Cambridge Elements ≡

Forensic Linguistics

Tim Grant

Aston University

Tim Grant is Professor of Forensic Linguistics, Director of the Aston Institute for Forensic Linguistics, and past president of the International Association of Forensic Linguists. His recent publications have focussed on online sexual abuse conversations including *Language and Online Identities: The Undercover Policing of Internet Sexual Crime* (with Nicci MacLeod, Cambridge, 2020).

Tim is one of the world's most experienced forensic linguistic practitioners and his case work has involved the analysis of abusive and threatening communications in many different contexts including investigations into sexual assault, stalking, murder, and terrorism. He also makes regular media contributions including presenting police appeals such as for the BBC Crimewatch programme.

Tammy Gales

Hofstra University

Tammy Gales is an Associate Professor of Linguistics and the Director of Research at the Institute for Forensic Linguistics, Threat Assessment, and Strategic Analysis at Hofstra University, New York. She has served on the Executive Committee for the International Association of Forensic Linguists (IAFL), is on the editorial board for the peer-reviewed journals *Applied Corpus Linguistics* and *Language and Law / Linguagem e Direito*, and is a member of the advisory board for the BYU Law and Corpus Linguistics group. Her research interests cross the boundaries of forensic linguistics and language and the law, with a primary focus on threatening communications. She has trained law enforcement agents from agencies across Canada and the U.S. and has applied her work to both criminal and civil cases.

About the Series

Elements in Forensic Linguistics provides high-quality accessible writing, bringing cutting-edge forensic linguistics to students and researchers as well as to practitioners in law enforcement and law. Elements in the series range from descriptive linguistics work, documenting a full range of legal and forensic texts and contexts; empirical findings and methodological developments to enhance research, investigative advice, and evidence for courts; and explorations into the theoretical and ethical foundations of research and practice in forensic linguistics.

Cambridge Elements ☰

Forensic Linguistics

Elements in the Series

The Idea of Progress in Forensic Authorship Analysis
Tim Grant

A full series listing is available at: www.cambridge.org/EIFL

Printed in the United States
by Baker & Taylor Publisher Services